WORLD PRE

C000015706

## A MUSICAL PLAY

# DONEGAL

## FRANK MCGUINNESS
## MUSIC BY KEVIN DOHERTY

Premiered on the <u>Abbey</u> stage
on Wednesday 12 October 2016

# ABBEY
# THEATRE
# AMHARCLANN
# NA MAINISTREACH

THE ABBEY THEATRE is Ireland's national theatre. It was founded by W.B. Yeats and Lady Augusta Gregory. Since it first opened its doors in 1904 the theatre has played a vital and often controversial role in the literary, social and cultural life of Ireland.

We place the writer and theatre-maker at the heart of all that we do, commissioning and producing exciting new work and creating discourse and debate on the political, cultural and social issues of the day. Our aim is to present great theatre in a national context so that the stories told on stage have a resonance with artists and audiences alike.

In 1905, the Abbey Theatre first toured internationally and continues to be an ambassador for Irish arts and culture worldwide.

Over the years, the Abbey Theatre has nurtured and premiered the work of major playwrights such as J.M. Synge and Sean O'Casey as well as contemporary classics from Sebastian Barry, Marina Carr, Bernard Farrell, Brian Friel, Thomas Kilroy, Frank McGuinness, Tom Mac Intyre, Tom Murphy, Mark O'Rowe and Billy Roche.

We support a new generation of Irish writers at the Abbey Theatre including Richard Dormer, Gary Duggan, Shaun Dunne, Stacey Gregg, Nancy Harris, David Ireland, Jimmy McAleavey, Owen McCafferty, Phillip McMahon Elaine Murphy, Sean P. Summers, Michael West and Carmel Winters.

None of this can happen without our audiences and our supporters. Annie Horniman provided crucial financial support to the Abbey in its first years. Many others have followed her lead by investing in and supporting our work.

We also gratefully acknowledge the financial support of the Arts Council.

Is í amharclann na mainistreach amharclann náisiúnta na hÉireann.

W.B. Yeats agus an Bantiarna Augusta Gregory a bhunaigh í. Riamh anall ón uair a osclaíodh a doirse i 1904, ghlac an amharclann ról an-tábhachtach agus, go minic, ról a bhí sách conspóideach, i saol liteartha, sóisialta agus cultúrtha na hÉireann.

Tá an scríobhneoir agus and t-amharclannóir i gcroílár a dhéanaimid anseo san amharclann, trí shaothar nua spreagúil a choimisiúnú agus a léiriú agus trí dhioscúrsa agus díospóireacht a chruthú i dtaobh cheisteanna polaitiúla, cultúrtha agus sóisialta na linne. Is í an aidhm atá againn amharclannaíochta den scoth a láithriú i gcomhthéacs náisiúnta ionas go mbeidh dáimh ag lucht ealaíne agus lucht féachana araon leis na scéalta a bhíonn á n-aithris ar an stáitse.

I 1905 is ea a chuaigh complacht Amharclann na Mainistreach ar camchuairt idirnáisiúnta den chéad uair agus leanann sí i gcónaí de bheith ina hambasadóir ar fud an domhain d'ealaíona agus cultúr na hÉireann.

In imeacht na mblianta, rinne Amharclann na Mainistreach saothar mórdhrámadóirí ar nós J.M. Synge agus Sean O'Casey a chothú agus a chéadléiriú, mar a rinne sí freisin i gcás clasaicí comhaimseartha ó dhrámadóirí amhail Sebastian Barry, Marina Carr, Bernard Farrell, Brian Friel, Thomas Kilroy, Frank McGuinness, Tom Mac Intyre, Tom Murphy, Mark O'Rowe agus Billy Roche.

Tugaimid tacaíocht chomh maith don ghlúin nua Scríbhneoirí Éireannacha in Amharclann na Mainistreach, lena n-áirítear Richard Dormer, Gary Duggan, Shaun Dunne, Stacey Gregg, Nancy Harris, David Ireland, Jimmy McAleavey, Owen McCafferty, Phillip McMahon, Elaine Murphy, Sean P. Summers, Michael West agus Carmel Winters.

Ní féidir aon ní den chineál sin a thabhairt i gcrích gan ár lucht féachana agus ár lucht tacaíochta. Sholáthair Annie Horniman tacaíocht airgid ríthábhachtach don Mhainistir siar i mblianta tosaigh na hamharclainne. Lean iliomad daoine eile an dea-shampla ceannródaíochta sin uaithi ó shin trí infheistíocht a dhéanamh inár gcuid oibre agus tacaíocht a thabhairt dúinn.

Táimid fíor bhuíoch don tacaíocht airgeadais atá le fail ón Chomhairle Ealaíon.

# A MUSICAL PLAY

# DONEGAL

## FRANK MCGUINNESS
## MUSIC BY KEVIN DOHERTY

CAST (IN ALPHABETICAL ORDER)

| | |
|---|---|
| *Magdalene Carolan* | Deirdre Donnelly |
| *Jackie Day* | Killian Donnelly |
| *Hugo Day* | John Kavanagh |
| *Conor Day* | Frank Laverty |
| *Irene Day* | Siobhan McCarthy |
| *Liam Brogan* | Keith McErlean |
| *Triona Brogan* | Ruth McGill |
| *Joanne Carolan* | Eleanor Methven |
| *Liza Field* | Megan Riordan |

MUSICIANS (IN ALPHABETICAL ORDER)

| | |
|---|---|
| *Pedal steel/Banjo/Guitar* | Paul Brennan |
| *Band Leader/Keyboards/Accordion* | James Delaney |
| *Drums/Percussion* | Jason Duffy |
| *Alto Saxophone/Clarinet* | Kenneth Edge |
| *Bass/Guitar* | Jack Maher |
| *Guitar* | Conor O'Farrell-Brady |

| | |
|---|---|
| *Writer* | Frank McGuinness |
| *Composer* | Kevin Doherty |
| *Director* | Conall Morrison |
| *Musical Director and Arranger* | Conor Linehan |
| *Set Designer* | Liam Doona |
| *Costume Designer* | Joan O'Clery |
| *Lighting Designer* | Ben Ormerod |
| *Sound Designer* | Alexis Nealon |
| *Audio Visual Designer* | Arnim Friess |
| *Movement Director* | Muirne Bloomer |
| *Assistant Director* | Conor Bagley |
| *Voice Director* | Andrea Ainsworth |
| *Casting Director* | Kelly Phelan |
| *Literary Manager* | Jessica Traynor |
| *Stage Manager* | Brendan Galvin |
| *Deputy Stage Manager* | Tara Furlong |
| *Assistant Stage Manager* | Stephen Dempsey |
| *Hair and Make-Up* | Val Sherlock |
| *Set Construction* | Ed Rourke, John Finnegan & Shane Kenny |
| *Scenic Artist* | Bellhouse Scenic Studio |
| *Photography* | Peter Rowen |
| *Graphic Design* | Zero-G |
| *Sign Language Interpreter* | Caroline O'Leary |
| *Audio Description* | Bríd Ní Ghruagáin & Máirín Harte |
| *Captioning* | Ruth McCreery |

Audio described and captioned performances are provided by Arts and Disability Ireland with funding from the Arts Council/An Chomhairle Ealaíon.

There will be one interval of 20 minutes.

Please note that the text of the play which appears in this volume may be changed during the rehearsal process and appear in a slightly altered form in performance.

SPECIAL THANKS TO
John Anderson at Conference Services and Cieran Kelly, Donegal GAA

# BIOGRAPHIES

*Writer*
Frank McGuinness

*Composer*
Kevin Doherty

*Cast*
Deirdre Donnelly
Killian Donnelly
John Kavanagh
Frank Laverty
Siobhan McCarthy
Keith McErlean
Ruth McGill
Eleanor Methven
Megan Riordan

*Musicians*
Paul Brennan
James Delaney
Jason Duffy
Kenneth Edge
Jack Maher
Conor O'Farrell-Brady

*Director*
Conall Morrison

*Musical Director
& Arranger*
Conor Linehan

*Set Designer*
Liam Doona

*Costume Designer*
Joan O'Clery

*Lighting Designer*
Ben Ormerod

*Sound Designer*
Alexis Nealon

*Audio Visual
Design*
Arnim Friess

*Movement
Director*
Muirne Bloomer

*Assistant Director*

FRANK HAS A long association with the Abbey Theatre. *Observe the Sons of Ulster Marching Towards the Somme* premiered there in 1985 and won the London Evening Standard Most Promising Playwright Award, the Rooney Prize for Irish Literature, Harvey's Best Play Award, the Cheltenham Literary Prize, the Plays and Players Award, the Ewart – Briggs Peace Prize and the London Fringe Award. His other plays at the Abbey Theatre include *The Hanging Gardens*, his dramatization of James Joyce's *The Dead*, an adaptation of Ibsen's *John Gabriel Borkman*, *Dolly West's Kitchen* (also Old Vic, London, nominated for an Olivier Award 2001), *The Bird Sanctuary*, *Lorca's Yerma*, *The Factory Girls*, *Carthaginians* (also Hampstead Theatre, London) and *Baglady*. Other theatre work includes *Innocence* and *The Bread Man* (Gate Theatre), *Gates of Gold* (Gate Theatre and Finborough Theatre, London), *Someone Who'll Watch Over Me*, nominated for a Tony Award (Hampstead Theatre, West End and Broadway), Winner of the New York Critics Circle Award and the Writers Guild Award for Best Play, *Mutabilitie* (National Theatre, London), *Speaking Like Magpies* and *Mary and Lizzie* (Royal Shakespeare Company), *There Came a Gypsy Riding* (Almeida Theatre, London), *Greta Garbo Came to Donegal* (Tricycle Theatre, London), *The Match Box* (Galway Arts Festival, Tricycle Theatre, London and Liverpool Playhouse) and *Crocodile* (Sky Arts Live and Riverside Studios). Frank's widely performed adaptations of classic plays include Ibsen's *Rosmersholm*, Brecht's *The Caucasian Chalk Circle* and Sophocles' *Oedipus* (National Theatre, London), Brecht's *The Threepenny Opera* (Gate Theatre), *Peer Gynt* (Gate Theatre, Royal Shakespeare Company, international tour and National Theatre, London), Chekhov's *Three Sisters* (Gate Theatre and Royal Court), *Hedda Gabler* (Roundabout, Broadway), *Uncle Vanya* (Field Day Production), *A Doll's House* (Playhouse Theatre, Broadway), Winner of the Tony Award for Best Revival and the Outer Critics Circle Award, de Molina's *Damned by Despair*, Racine's *Phaedra* (Donmar Warehouse), Sophocles' *Electra*, nominated for a Tony Award (Chichester, Donmar Warehouse and Barrymore Theatre, Broadway), Ostrovsky's *The Storm* (Almeida Theatre, London), Strindberg's *Miss Julie* (Theatre Royal Haymarket, London), Euripides' *Hecuba* (Donmar Warehouse), a dramatization of du Maurier's *Rebecca* (David Pugh productions and UK tour), Ibsen's *Ghosts* (Bristol Old Vic and Duchess Theatre London), *The Lady from the Sea* (Arcola Theatre) and Euripides' *Helen* (Shakespeare's Globe). Film and television work includes *Dancing at Lughnasa*, *Talk of Angels*, *Scout*, *The Hen House*, *The Stranger* (BAFTA nomination), *A Short Stay in Switzerland*, Broadcast Prize and BAFTA Nomination and *A Song for Jenny* (BBC). Frank lectures in English at University College Dublin. He was born in Buncrana, Co. Donegal, and now lives in Dublin.

## KEVIN DOHERTY

COMPOSER

THIS IS KEVIN'S debut at the Abbey Theatre. He has played music professionally since the age of 19. He is a member of the traditional band Four Men and A Dog and has recorded six albums with them, most recently *And the Band Played On*, to mark 25 years together. Kevin recorded three solo albums and one album with the band Telegraph. He is currently working with them on their second album which is due out in the autumn. His songs have been recorded by Levon Helm, Rick Danko and Mary Black. Kevin provided the music for the film *Watermelon* (Blinder Films). Kevin was born in Buncrana, Co. Donegal and now lives in Dublin.

## DEIRDRE DONNELLY

MAGDALENE CAROLAN

DEIRDRE'S PREVIOUS WORK at the Abbey Theatre includes *Conservatory, Shush, Bookworms* (2012 and 2010), *An Ideal Husband, The Big House, The Crucible, Seven Jewish Children, A Month in the Country, Da, She Stoops to Folly, Drama at Inish, Too Late for Logic, You Can't Take It With You, Not I, All My Sons, Scenes from an Album, The Blue Macushla, The Well of the Saints, Catchpenny Twist, Tarry Flynn, The Vicar of Wakefield, Twelfth Night, The Gathering, The Scatterin', Blood Wedding, The Whiteheaded Boy* and *In the Shadow of the Glen*.

Other theatre work includes *The Importance of Being Earnest, Pride and Prejudice, Bedroom Farce, A Woman of No Importance, Little Women, Jane Eyre, Death of a Salesman, Les Liaisons Dangereuses, Aristocrats, Blithe Spirit* and *Agnes of God* (Gate Theatre), *The Scythe and the Sunset, Bedtime Story, Talk to Me Like the Rain, Old Times, She Stoops to Conquer, The J. Arthur Maginnis Story, As You Like It* and *Thieves Carnival* (Irish Theatre Company), *A Dream of Autumn*, Irish Times Theatre Award nomination for Best Supporting Actress 2005 and *Down Onto Blue* (Rough Magic Theatre Company), *Boesman and Lena* (Field Day Theatre Company), *Play it Again, Sam, Crooked in a Car-Seat* and *Private Lives* (Gemini), *Chapter Two* (Olympia Theatre), *A Delicate Balance* (Focus Theatre), *Nuts and Bolts*, one-woman play (Bewley's Café Theatre and Viking Theatre), *Over the River and Through the Woods* (Andrew's Lane Theatre) and *There Came A Gypsy Riding* (Livin' Dred Theatre Company). Film and television work includes *Striking Out* (Blinder Films/RTÉ), *The Frankenstein Chronicles* (Rainmark Films/ITV), *Quirke* (Element Pictures/BBC), *Homemade* (ParkFilms), *Amber* (Amber Film Productions), *Cracks* (Scott-Free Productions), six seasons of *Ballykissangel* (World Productions/BBC), *Legend* (Icebox Productions/RTÉ), *The Irish RM* (Channel 4/RTÉ), *The Clinic* (Parallel Productions/RTÉ), *Fair City, Molloy, Thou Shalt Not Kill, Miracles and Miss Langan, The Last of the Summer* and *The Riordans* (RTÉ), *Goodbye Darling* (Fantastic Films), *Fatal Lovers* (Lapaca Films), *The Fantasist* (ITC Films), *Garage* (Element Pictures), *Da Capo* (New Ripple Productions), *Attracta* and *Criminal Conversation* (BAC Films) and *Runway One* (BBC). Radio dramas include *Down Onto Blue, A Grand Reunion, Gentleman and Players, The Burning of Bridget Cleary, No Hate Going to Loss, Nomads, The Fishmonger's Wife, Border Crossing, Moving-In Day, The Intimacy Incentive, The House on Shareni Street, Oblivion* and *The Disappeared* (RTÉ), *Autumn Sunshine, Rotunda Blue, Say No to Shantonagh* and *The Hill Bachelors* (BBC).

# KILLIAN DONNELLY
### JACKIE DAY

THIS IS KILLIAN's debut at the Abbey Theatre. Other theatre work includes Huey Calhoun in *Memphis* (Shaftesbury Theatre), for which he received a 2015 Olivier Award Nomination for Best Actor in a Musical, Deco in *The Commitments* (Palace Theatre) directed by Jamie Lloyd, Tony in *Billy Elliot the Musical* (Victoria Palace Theatre), Raoul in *The Phantom of the Opera* (Her Majesty's Theatre), Enjolras in *Les Misérables* (Queen's Theatre), before which he understudied and played the roles of Jean Valjean and Javert, Collins in *Michael Collins* (Cork Opera House), *Sweeney Todd* (Gate Theatre, Dublin), Ethan Girard in *The Full Monty* (Olympia Theatre), Tony in *West*

*Side Story* (The Solstice), Declan in *The Wireman* (Gaiety Theatre) and Rod in *Singin' in the Rain* (Olympia Theatre). Workshops include Frankie in *Angela's Ashes*, Pink in *The Wall* directed by Simon McBurney and Deco in *The Commitments*. Concerts include *West End Musicals* (Halle Orchestra - Bridgewater Hall, Manchester), *The Phantom of the Opera 25th Anniversary* (Royal Albert Hall), Courfeyrac in *Les Misérables 25th Anniversary* (02 Arena), *You Should Be Dancing* (National Concert Hall, Dublin) and *Les Misérables* (Bournemouth Symphony Orchestra - Isle of Wight). Film and television work includes *Les Misérables Chorus* in The 85th Academy Awards (Dolby Theatre, Los Angeles), Combeferre in *Les Misérables* (Working Title Films) directed by Tom Hooper, *Showbands* (BBC), *The Last Furlong, Bachelors Walk, The Late Late Show, Open House* (RTÉ) and *The Tudors* (BBC). Most recently, Killian starred as Charlie Price in the original London production of *Kinky Boots* (Adelphi Theatre), for which he received a 2016 Olivier Award Nomination for Best Actor in a Musical and was shortlisted at the 2015 Evening Standard Theatre Awards for Best Musical Performance. Killian is a Member of the PMA.

## JOHN KAVANAGH
### HUGO DAY

JOHN WAS A MEMBER of the Abbey Theatre Company for ten years. His previous work at the Abbey Theatre includes *A Midsummer Night's Dream*, *Aristocrats*, *King Lear*, *John Gabriel Borkman*, *Macbeth*, *The Comedy of Errors*, *Big Love*, *Fool For Love*, *The Cavalcaders*, *The Plough and the Stars*, *Observe the Sons of Ulster Marching towards the Somme*, *Da*, *A Life*, *Wonderful Tennessee*, *King of the Castle*, *Translations*, *All My Sons*, *Faith Healer* and *Aristocrats*. Other theatre work includes *The Speckled People*, *A View From the Bridge*, *Da*, *See You Next Tuesday*, *Eccentricities of a Nightingale*, *As You Like It*, *The Homecoming*, *Dublin Carol*, *Deep Blue Sea* and *Juno and the Paycock* (Gate Theatre) and *The Making of 'Tis Pity She's a Whore* (Project Arts Centre). Musicals include *Jacques Brel is Alive and Well*, *Cabaret*, *Guys and Dolls*, *The Pirates of Penzance* and *Les Misérables*. Film and television work includes *Florence Foster Jenkins* (Querty Films/Pathé), *The Great Wide Open* (Pitchmark Ltd), *In Secret* (LD Entertainment), *The Invisible Woman* (Headline Pictures), *The Stag* (Irish Film Board), *The Tiger's Tail* (Fern Gully Tales), *The Black Dahlia* (Millennium Films), *Alexander* (Intermedia), *Dancing at Lughnasa* (Ferndale Films), *Sharpe* (Celtic Films Entertainment), *Into the West* (Channel 4 Films), *The Butcher Boy* (Geffen Pictures), *Braveheart* (Kon Productions), *Circle of Friends* (Price Entertainment), *Jack Taylor* (TV3), *Titanic: Blood and Steel* (Epos Films), *Father & Son* (Left Bank Pictures), *The Clinic* (Parallel Films), *Holby City*, *Arise and Go Now*, *The Tudors*, *Anytime Now*, *Rebel Heart*, *Vicious Circle*, *Shadow of a Gunman*, *Dr. Findlay* and *Bad Company* (BBC), *Fools of Fortune* (Working Title Films), *Caught in a Free State* (Granada Television), *Inspector George Gently* (Irish Film Board), *Therese Raquin* (Liddell Entertainment) and *Vikings* (VK Productions for MGM and History Channel).

## FRANK LAVERTY
### CONOR DAY

FRANK'S PREVIOUS WORK at the Abbey Theatre includes *The House*, *Iphegenia at Aulis*, *Portia Coughlan*, *Away Alone*, *Sour Grapes*, *The Hamlet Project*, *The Countess Cathleen*, *Silverlands*, *The Winter Thief*, *On the Outside/On the Inside*, *The Comedy of Errors*, *Famine*, *Translations* and *Aristocrats*. Other theatre work includes *All That Fall* (Bristol Old Vic and Wilton's Music Hall, London), *A Particle of Dread* (The Playhouse, Belfast), *A Skull in Connemara*, *Philadelphia, Here I Come!*, *Silverlands*, *Song of the Yellow Bittern* and *At the Black Pigs Dyke* (Druid Theatre Company), *The Rivals* (Southwark Playhouse), *The Beauty Queen of Leenane* (Young Vic Theatre and Gaiety Theatre), *A Whistle in the Dark* (Royal Exchange), *The Playboy of the Western World* (Old Vic Theatre), *Words of Advice for Young People* and *Dream of Autumn* (Rough Magic), *The*

*Beauty Queen of Leenane* and *The Belfry* (Livin' Dred Theatre Company). Film and television work includes *Rebel Heart* and *Doctors* (BBC), *Raw, Glenroe, On Home Ground, Love is the Drug, Stardust, An Gaeltacht, Pure Mule* and *Single-Handed* (RTÉ), *Casualty* (BBC), *Trouble in Paradise* (Great Western Films), *Teenage Cics* (Abú Media), *Noble* (Destiny Films), *All is By My Side* (Darko Entertainment), *Michael Collins* (Warner Bros Pictures), *The Abduction Club* (Gruber Films), *The Closer You Get* (Redwave Films) and *The General* (John Boorman Productions). Radio work includes *Farran at Bay* (BBC Radio 4), *Philadelphia, Here I Come!, O Go My Man* and *Oedipus* (RTÉ).

## SIOBHAN MCCARTHY
IRENE DAY

THIS IS SIOBHAN's debut at the Abbey Theatre. She appeared in the original West End productions of *Mamma Mia!* (Olivier Nominated for Best Actress Award), *Chess* and *Evita*. Other work in the West End includes *Sweeney Todd* (also at Harrington's Pie and Mash Shop), *Hairspray, Medea* (also USA Tour and Broadway), *Blood Brothers, Dancing at Lughnasa, On Your Toes, Les Misérables* and *Jesus Christ Superstar*. Other theatre work includes *Pure Imagination* (St James Theatre), *Richard III* (Nottingham/York Theatre Royal), *Company* (Southwark Playhouse), *The Drowsy Chaperone* (The Gatehouse), *Peter Pan* (Leicester Curve), *Bloodbath* (Edinburgh

Festival), *Days of Hope* (Kings Head Theatre), *Wonderful Tennessee* (Nottingham Playhouse), *One Glass Wall* (Theatre 503), *No Trams to Lime Street* (Liverpool Playhouse), *Zorro - The Musical* (Theatre Royal, Stratford) and *Jeanne* (Birmingham Rep Theatre). Television and film work includes *Bad Girls* (ITV), *Law and Order* (Kudos Film & TV), *Holby City* and *Lovejoy* (BBC), *All in the Game, All or Nothing at All* and *The Big Battalions* (Carnival Films), *Time's Fool* (Bakehouse Productions Ltd/Ekran) and *Horse Opera* (Initial Films). Siobhan was a member of the singing group Wall Street Crash.

## KEITH MCERLEAN
LIAM BROGAN

KEITH'S PREVIOUS WORK at the Abbey Theatre includes *Hedda Gabler, Aristocrats, The Colleen Bawn, Tartuffe, Lovers at Versaille, Down the Line, Portia Coughlan* and *Making History*. Other theatre work includes *On Raftery's Hill* (Druid), *We Ourselves* and *Studs* (Passion Machine), *Macbeth* (Upstate Theatre), *Cyrano De Bergerac* (Gate Theatre) and *Sky Road* (Theatre Royal). Film and television work includes *Flyboys* (Lionsgate Films), *Jump* (Blinder Films), *Swansong: The Story of Occi Byrne* and *Recoil* (Zanzibar Films), *When Brendan Met Trudy* (Deadly Films), *Tug* (Angelic Films), *Goldfish Memory* (Goldfish Films), *The Escapist* (Sky Pictures), *Trivia, RAW* and *Bachelors Walk* (RTÉ), *The Trial of the Century* (TV3), *Doctors* (BBC), *Touched by*

an *Angel* and *Blackwater Lightship*
(CBS Television), *Blood Cells* (Third
Films), *Sing Street* (Distressed
Films) and most recently *Vikings*
Series 5 (VK Productions for MGM
and the History Channel).

## RUTH MCGILL
TRIONA BROGAN

RUTH'S PREVIOUS WORK at the Abbey
Theatre includes *Twelfth Night,
Alice in Funderland, Christ Deliver
Us!, The Last Days of a Reluctant
Tyrant* and *The Cherry Orchard.*
Other theatre work includes *The
Threepenny Opera*, for which she
was nominated for Best Supporting
Actress Irish Times Theatre
Awards 2013 and *Sweeney Todd*
(Gate Theatre), *Dubliners, Freefall,*
nominated for Best Supporting
Actress Irish Times Theatre
Awards 2011 and *Cat on a Hot Tin
Roof* (The Corn Exchange), *Stoker*
(Ouroboros Theatre Company),
*Everybody Loves Sylvia, Fewer
Emergencies, The Drowned World,
The Illusion* and *Eeugh!topia*
(Randolph SD | The Company),
*Macbecks* (Olympia Theatre), *All
in the Timing* (Inis Theatre), *The
Turn of the Screw* (Storytellers),
*Can You Catch a Mermaid?*
(Pavilion Theatre), *Woyzeck*
(Rough Magic SEEDS) and *The
Shaughraun* (Albery Theatre,
London). Film and television
work includes *Miscalculation*
(Still Films), *Jack Taylor: Shot
Down* (Magma Productions),
*Damo & Ivor, Love/Hate* and
*The Clinic* (RTÉ), *Wonderhouse*
(Wonderhouse Productions),
*What Richard Did* (Element
Pictures) and *Leap Year* (Spyglass
Entertainment). Ruth is also a

singer-songwriter and is part of the
three-part harmony and musical
collective *The Evertides*. Ruth
graduated from the Professional
Acting Programme at the Samuel
Beckett Centre, Trinity College
Dublin.

## ELEANOR METHVEN
JOANNE CAROLAN

ELEANOR'S PREVIOUS WORK at the
Abbey Theatre includes *You Never
Can Tell, Major Barbara, The
House, Pygmalion, No Escape,
Christ Deliver Us!, The Recruiting
Officer, Saved*, Winner Irish Times
Theatre Award for Best Supporting
Actress 2007, *Homeland, The
Shape of Metal, The Wild Duck,
The Barbaric Comedies, Tartuffe*
and *Hamlet* (Abbey Theatre
and Lyric Theatre, Belfast co-
production). Other theatre work
includes *The Importance of Being
Earnest*, Winner Irish Times
Theatre Award for Best Supporting
Actress 2010, *Northern Star, Don
Carlos, Famished Castle, Plaza
Suite, Pentecost, Solemn Mass for
a Full Moon in Summer* (Rough
Magic Theatre Company), *Pride
and Prejudice* (Gate Theatre),
*The Last Days of Judas Iscariot*
(Making Strange Theatre
Company), *The Year of the Hiker*
(Druid), *Unravelling the Ribbon*
(Gúna Nua and Plan B), *Strandline*
(Fishamble: The New Play
Company), *Dancing at Lughnasa*,
Irish Times/ESB Award for Best
Actress 2002 (An Grianán),
*Weddins, Weeins and Wakes, The
Factory Girls, Conversations on
a Homecoming, The Shadow of
a Gunman* and *Macbeth* (Lyric

Theatre, Belfast), *Our Father* (Almeida Theatre), *Simpatico, Scenes from the Big Picture, Vincent River* and *Chilogy* (Prime Cut Productions), *Medea* (Siren Productions) and *Care* (WillFredd Theatre Company). Eleanor is co-founder of the award-winning Charabanc Theatre Company. In 1993 she received an EMA Best Actress Award for her work with the company, where she was Co-Artistic Director until 1995. Film and television work includes *The Clinic, DDU, Amber* and *Love is the Drug,* IFTA nomination for Best Supporting Actress 2005 (RTÉ), *An Crisis* (TG4), *A Love Divided, Falling for a Dancer* and *The Snapper* (BBC), *The Boxer* (Universal Pictures), *Titanic: Blood and Steel* (Antena 3 Films), *Mad about Mambo* (First City Features Ltd), *The Ambassador* (Ecosse Films), *Disco Pigs* (Temple Film and TV Productions Ltd), *The Return* (Octagon Films), *The Baby War* (Granada Television), *Becoming Jane* (HanWay Films), *Sensations* (Blinder Films), *The Ice Cream Girls* (Left Bank Pictures), *Reign* (CBS/Octagon Films) and *The Truth Commissioner* (BT9 Films.)

## PAUL BRENNAN
PEDAL STEEL/BANJO/GUITAR

THIS IS PAUL'S debut at the Abbey Theatre. He is a well-known musician on the Irish country music scene playing guitar, pedal steel guitar, harmonica and fiddle. His guitar influences range from Jimmy Page to Chet Atkins. Paul developed an interest in the pedal steel guitar and has studied with some of the finest Nashville based players. Paul is a key member of the Irish Pedal Steel Guitar Association and regularly performs at their festivals alongside some the finest musicians from around the world. He has played with many of the top Irish country artists including Larry Cunningham, Mick Flavin, Noel Cassidy and Robert Mizzel on stage, in the recording studio and on television. He is originally from Athlone but now lives in Dublin.

## JAMES DELANEY
BAND LEADER/KEYBOARDS/ ACCORDION

THIS IS JAMES' debut at the Abbey Theatre. He played in the blues and rock scene in Dublin and in the eighties joined Clannad with whom he composed music for the ITV series *Robin of Sherwood.* Since then he has collaborated with many other artists including Kevin Doherty and Davey Spillane. He has played on countless recordings and toured or recorded with the likes of Chuck Berry, Paul Brady, Mary Coughlan, Four Men and a Dog, Andrew Strong, Rory Gallagher, Van Morrison, Henry McCullagh, Máirtín O' Connor, Sharon Shannon, Steve Earl Jackson Brown and Dessie O' Halloran. Currently he is writing and recording with his band Los Paradiso.

## JASON DUFFY
DRUMS/PERCUSSION

THIS IS JASON's debut at the Abbey Theatre. He has been playing drums since the age of twelve. He comes from the famous Duffy Circus family and over the last twenty years has gone on tour and recorded with many artists such as Michael Flatley's *Lord of the Dance*, Feet of Flames and Celtic Tiger, The Corrs, Sharon Shannon, Bono, Paul Brady, Imelda May, The Waterboys, Shane MacGowan, Declan O'Rourke, Jeff Beck, Damien Dempsey, Picture House and many more.

## KENNETH EDGE
ALTO SAXOPHONE/CLARINET

THIS IS KENNETH's debut at the Abbey Theatre. A saxophonist, he is one of Ireland's leading and most innovative musicians. He studied with Sydney Egan in Dublin, John Harle in London and Jean-Marie Londeix in Bordeaux. He began his musical career by winning the RTÉ Young Musician of the Future competition in 1983. He was the original Saxophonist for *Riverdance* and Solo Clarinettist for the original Broadway production of Boublil and Schoenberg's *The Pirate Queen*. Kenneth's saxophone playing has inspired many leading composers to write new works for him, including John Buckley's *Concerto for Alto Sax and String Orchestra*. He is the featured saxophone soloist on two movie soundtracks, *A Rage in Harlem* and *The Grifters*, by the American film composer Elmer Bernstein. He composed the score for *Touch Me* by CoisCéim Dance Theatre, which premiered at Project Arts Centre.

## JACK MAHER
BASS/GUITAR

THIS IS JACK's debut at the Abbey Theatre. He is a guitarist, musician, multi-instrumentalist and singer songwriter. He has worked with many leading artists in the music scene around Ireland and abroad including Sharon Shannon, Declan O'Rourke, Lisa Lambe, Mundy, Damien Dempsey, Eddi Reader, Van Morrison, Gerry Fish, Camille O'Sullivan and Shane MacGowan.

## CONOR O'FARRELL-BRADY
GUITAR

THIS IS CONOR's debut at the Abbey Theatre. A guitar player, he has recorded and performed with many local and international artists and producers, and is currently based at Camden Recording Studios. Conor began playing with Dublin band The Blades and is currently working with both The Drays and The Bronagh Gallagher Band. In addition to production and recording work he teaches guitar techniques occasionally at BIMM Music College.

## CONALL MORRISON
### DIRECTOR

CONALL'S PREVIOUS WORK at the Abbey Theatre includes *Tina's Idea of Fun, You Never Can Tell, She Stoops to Conquer, Sive, Translations, The Last Days of a Reluctant Tyrant, The Big House, The Importance of Being Earnest, The Bacchae of Baghdad, Hamlet* (a co-production with The Lyric Theatre, Belfast), his own adaptation of Patrick Kavanagh's *Tarry Flynn* (also at the Lyttleton, National Theatre, London), Boucicault's *The Colleen Bawn* (also Lyttleton Theatre), *The Freedom of the City, The Tempest, The House, A Whistle in the Dark, Ariel, In a Little World of Our Own, As the Beast Sleeps, Twenty Grand, Savoy* and a triple bill comprising *The Dandy Dolls, Purgatory* and *Riders to the Sea/Chun na Farraige Síos*. Other theatre work includes *Guaranteed!* and *Bailed Out!* (Fishamble: The New Play Company), *Beginning to End* (Happy Days Beckett Festival), *Borstal Boy* (Gaiety Theatre and Verdant Productions), *Scenes from the Big Picture* (Prime Cut Productions), *Conquest of the South Pole, The Marlboro Man, Emma, Measure for Measure, Macbeth, Kvetch* and his own adaptation of *Antigone*. For the Lyric Theatre, Belfast he directed *Smiley, The Crucible, The Playboy of the Western World, Dancing at Lughnasa, Juno and the Paycock, Conversations on a Homecoming* and *Ghosts*. He directed *Martin Guerre* for Cameron Mackintosh, touring England and America. He directed the musical *Ludwig II* at the Festspielhaus Neuschwanstein, Germany and *La Traviata* (English National Opera). Productions for the Royal Shakespeare Company include *Macbeth* and *The Taming of the Shrew*. His production of *Richard II*, in Arabic, played in Jericho, Ramallah, Dubai and The Globe Theatre. For the Playhouse Theatre he directed *Re-energize* by Gary Mitchell, with music by The Undertones, as part of the programme for Derry City of Culture. His own plays include *Rough Justice, Hard to Believe* and *Green, Orange and Pink*.

## CONOR LINEHAN
### MUSICAL DIRECTOR AND ARRANGER

CONOR'S PREVIOUS WORK at the Abbey Theatre includes scores for *Othello, You Never Can Tell, She Stoops to Conquer, Sive, The Risen People, King Lear, The Dead, The Plough and the Stars* (2012 and 2010), *Translations, Arrah na Pogue, The Last Days of a Reluctant Tyrant, Only an Apple, Marble, The School for Scandal, Homeland, The Cherry Orchard, The Tempest, She Stoops to Conquer, The Wake, Saint Joan, The Colleen Bawn* and *Love in the Title*. Other theatre work includes *Borstal Boy* (Gaiety Theatre), *Sleeping Beauty, The Playboy of the Western World, The Crucible, Carthaginians* and *A Doll's House* (Lyric Theatre, Belfast), *Medea, The Making of 'Tis Pity She's a Whore* and *The Lulu House* (Siren Productions), *The Cordelia Dream, The Taming of the Shrew, Macbeth, Two Gentlemen of Verona, Edward the Third, Loveplay* and *Luminosity* (Royal Shakespeare Company),

*Peer Gynt* and *The Playboy of the Western World* (National Theatre, London), *American Buffalo, A View From the Bridge* and *Long Day's Journey into Night* (Gate Theatre), *Dubliners, Freefall, Everyday* and *Dublin by Lamplight* (The Corn Exchange), *The Crock of Gold* and *Antigone* (Storytellers), *Mermaids* (CoisCéim Dance Theatre), *Rebecca* (David Pugh), *Rosencrantz and Guildenstern are Dead* and *Four Knights at Knaresborough* (West Yorkshire Playhouse), *The Hypochondriac, Tartuffe, Intemperance, The Mollusc* and *The Mayor of Zalamea* (Everyman, Liverpool) and *Twelfth Night* (Thelma Holt Productions). Conor has written many scores for radio. In addition Conor works extensively as a concert pianist and has performed with all of Ireland's major orchestras, premiered concertos by Ronan Guilfoyle and Don Ray as well as performing extensive solo and chamber music repertoire. He wrote a piano concerto for the Royal Irish Academy of Music Big Band and Therese Fahy, which was premiered at the National Concert Hall and subsequently performed in America and Ireland. He toured the United States with the Dublin Philharmonic performing concertos by Beethoven and Shostakovich. Conor is on the piano faculty of the Royal Irish Academy of Music. With Ben Delaney of the Abbey Theatre, Conor won the 2010 Irish Times Theatre Award for Best Sound Design for *The Last Days of a Reluctant Tyrant* as well as being nominated in the Judges Special Award category 'for setting the standard for original composition in theatre.'

## LIAM DOONA
### SET DESIGNER

LIAM'S PREVIOUS WORK at the Abbey Theatre includes *You Never Can Tell, She Stoops to Conquer, Conservatory* and *Gulliver's Travels*. Other theatre work includes *Smiley* (Lyric Theatre Belfast), *The Bloody Irish* (Helix Theatre and PBS Television), *The Field* and *Borstal Boy* (Gaiety Theatre), *Best Man* (Everyman Palace Theatre), *The Death of Harry Leon* (Ouroboros Theatre Company), *To Kill a Mockingbird* and *Romeo and Juliet* (York Theatre Royal), *The White Album* (Nottingham Playhouse), *Boys Stuff* (Sheffield Crucible) and *The Rivals, Endgame, The Merchant of Venice* and *The Seagull* (Compass Theatre). Liam's work was featured at The Victoria and Albert Museum, London, as part of a quadrennial review of British stage design. His work can be seen in *2D 3D* (2002) and *Collaborators* (2007), published by SBTD. His academic writing is featured in *A Reader in Scenography* and *Designers Shakespeare*, both published by Routledge. He is currently working on a biography of Irish designer, Sean Kenny. Liam is Head of the Department of Design and Visual Arts at Dun Laoghaire Institute of Art, Design and Technology.

## JOAN O'CLERY
COSTUME DESIGNER

JOAN'S PREVIOUS WORK at the Abbey Theatre includes *Othello, You Never Can Tell, She Stoops to Conquer, Sive, The Hanging Gardens, Major Barbara, Translations, The Plough and the Stars, Christ Deliver Us!, The Last Days of a Reluctant Tyrant, The Importance of Being Earnest, Hamlet, A Doll's House, The Wild Duck, Lolita* (Irish Times Theatre Award for Best Costume Design 2002), *A Whistle in the Dark* and *The Colleen Bawn*. Other theatre work includes *Macbeth* (Globe Theatre, London), *A View from the Bridge, Wuthering Heights, A Streetcar Named Desire, Arcadia, Boston Marriage, Endgame, Watt, Celebration, God of Carnage, Oleanna, Molly Sweeney, An Enemy of the People, The Pinter Festival,* Irish Times Theatre Award for Best Costume Design 1997 (Gate Theatre), *The Train, Peer Gynt* Irish Times Theatre Award for Best Costume Design 2012 (Rough Magic Theatre Company), *The Girl Who Forgot To Sing Badly* (The Ark/Theatre Lovett), *DruidMurphy* (Druid Theatre Company), *The Crucible, Dancing at Lughnasa* (Lyric Theatre, Belfast), *The Taming of the Shrew* and *Macbeth* (Royal Shakespeare Company Stratford and West End). Dance and Opera work includes *The Rite of Spring* and *Swept* (CoisCéim Dance Theatre), *Scheherezade* (Ballet Ireland), *Turandot* and *Dead Man Walking* (Opera Ireland), *Aida* (Lyric Opera), *La Traviata* (English National Opera at the London Coliseum) and *Moses* (St Gallen, Switzerland). Film and television work includes *Snap and Swansong, The Story of Occi Byrne* and *King of the Travellers* (both IFTA nominated for Best Costume Design), *The Trial of the Century* and *The Nation Holds Its Breath*.

## BEN ORMEROD
LIGHTING DESIGNER

BEN'S PREVIOUS WORK at the Abbey Theatre includes *You Never Can Tell, She Stoops to Conquer, Translations, The Big House, The Importance of Being Earnest, The Freedom of the City* (also New York), *The Colleen Bawn, The House, The Wake* and *Made in China*. Ben has worked extensively with The Royal Shakespeare Company, The National Theatre, English Touring Theatre and Propeller. In the West End his productions have included *Mrs Henderson Presents, Onassis, Macbeth* and *Zorro!*. Other theatre work includes *The Libertine, Trouble In Mind, The One That Got Away, Mrs Henderson Presents, Things We Do For Love, Intimate Apparel, The Spanish Golden Age* and *Iphigenia* (Bath), *Death of a Comedian* (Soho), *The Herbal Bed* (Clwyd), *This Restless House, Hamlet* and *King Lear* (Glasgow Citizens), *Fings Aint Wot They Used T'be* (Stratford East), *The Colleen Bawn* (Druid), *In the Next Room* (St James), *The Beauty Queen of Leenane* (Druid/West End/Broadway/Sydney/Toronto), *The Crucible* (Lyric Theatre, Belfast) and *Dimetos* (Donmar). Ben's many opera and dance credits include *Tannhäuser,*

*Tristan und Isolde* and *Der Ring Des Nibelungen* (Longborough), *Casse Noisette* for Grand Théâtre Genève and *La Traviata* for Danish National Opera as well as productions for Scottish Opera, ENO, Buxton Opera Festival, Academia Santa Cecilia Rome, Ballet Gulbenkian, Rambert, Candoco and Walker Dance Park Music. Ben is also lighting designer for the Calico Museum of Textiles, Ahmedabad, directed Athol Fugard's *Dimetos* (Gate, London) and adapted four films from Kieslowski's *Dekalog* for E15.

## ALEXIS NEALON
SOUND DESIGNER

THIS IS ALEXIS' debut at the Abbey Theatre. He is an Irish sound engineer and has worked with music and theatre ensembles for over 20 years, at home and abroad. From electro-acoustic music concerts, recordings and broadcasts, through international ethnic virtuosi performances, he has materialised and enhanced their artistic needs and visions. Previous theatre designs and compositions have included *[Like] Silver* (I.M.D.T.), *Knots* (CoisCéim Dance Theatre), *Drinking Dust* (Broken Talkers/Junk Ensemble), *James, Son of James* (Fabulous Beast), *The Train* (Rough Magic Theatre Company) and many more. He has worked with many music acts including The Quiet Music Ensemble, The Bonny Men, The High Kings, Crash Ensemble, Lorcán Mac Mathuna, Antibalas Afrobeat Orchestra and countless others. Originally a guitarist,

he developed synthesizer and computer skills to realise original compositions. More recently, he became an associate of Gradcam, a Doctoral level, practice-based music research group. Alexis holds a Masters in Music and Media Technology from Trinity College Dublin.

## ARNIM FRIESS
AUDIO VISUAL DESIGNER

THIS IS ARNIM's debut at the Abbey Theatre. He specialises in designing dynamic performance environments, blending lighting, video, photography and motion graphics. His lighting and projection designs have been seen not only in theatres around the world, but also in a zoo, a monastery, an abandoned pub and in a cave. Recent designs include *Look Back in Anger* and *Jinny* (Derby Theatre), *Alice in Wonderland* (Polka Theatre), *Ghosts in the Wall* (Royal Shakespeare Company), *Piaf* and *Gypsy* (The Curve Leicester), *Leviathan* (Matadero Madrid), *Grandpa in my Pocket* and *The White Album* (Nottingham Playhouse), *Wander* (Jockey Club Theatre, Hong Kong, the National Holocaust Memorial Day), *The Rememberers* (Birmingham Rep), *Lucky Seven* (Hampstead Theatre), *Looking for JJ* (Pilot Theatre at the Unicorn), *One Night in November* (Belgrade Theatre, Coventry), *The Suicide* and *An Inspector Calls* (Theatre Clwyd) and a roof of light for Coventry Cathedral's Blitz commemoration.

## MUIRNE BLOOMER
MOVEMENT DIRECTOR

MUIRNE'S PREVIOUS WORK at the Abbey Theatre includes *You Never Can Tell, She Stoops to Conquer, The Dandy Dolls, The Tempest, Drama at Inish, Cavalcaders* and *A Doll's House*. Recent theatre work includes Laochra for GAA 2016 commemoration, *The Train* (Rough Magic Theatre Company, Dublin Theatre Festival 2015) and *Rigoletto* (Opera Ireland with Selina Cartmell). Other theatre work includes *Borstal Boy* (Gaiety Theatre), *Pageant, As You Are* (CoisCéim Dance Theatre) and *The Ballet Ruse* (with Emma O'Kane), *Ssh we have a Plan, Nivelli's War, Duck Death and the Tulip, The Incredible Book Eating Boy, Egg, A Spell of Cold Weather* (Cahoots NI), *Gulliver's Travels* (National Youth Theatre), *Little Women* and *Arcadia* (The Gate Theatre), *Dancing at Lughnasa* (The Gate Theatre, An Grianán Theatre, The Bucharest National Theatre and Second Age), *Wallflowering, Hue and Cry, Maisy Daly's Rainbow* (Tall Tales), *Can You Catch a Mermaid* (Pavilion Theatre), *The Death of Harry Leon* (Ouroboros), *The Merchant of Venice* (Second Age) and *The Lulu House* and *The Making of 'Tis a Pity She's a Whore* (Siren Productions). Television work includes *Rock Rivals* (UTV). Muirne also choreographed the Special Olympics Opening Ceremony in Belfast in 2005. She jointly devised *A Dash of Colour* (Special Olympics Croke Park 2004), *Intimate Details* and *Golf Swing* (Opening Ceremony Ryder Cup 2006) and the opening ceremony for UEFA League Final (Aviva Stadium 2011). Muirne directed Macnas at the Galway Arts Festival Parade in 2004 and 2005. She has directed a pageant for St Patrick's Festival annually since 2004 including the City Fusion and Brighter Futures project for 2016.

## CONOR BAGLEY
ASSISTANT DIRECTOR

THIS IS CONOR'S debut at the Abbey Theatre. Previously, Conor directed *Dancing at Lughnasa* and *Shining City* (Yale). He was assistant director on *Other Desert Cities* (Theatre Workshop of Nantucket), *Die Fledermaus* and *The Real Inspector Hound* (Yale) and was the production assistant on *The Weir* (Irish Repertory Theatre, New York). A graduate of Yale University, Conor's acting credits include Rothko in *Red*, Ram's Dad in *Heathers: The Musical*, George in *All My Sons*, Marvin/Mort in *California Suite* and many others. He is recipient of the 2016 V. Browne Irish Prize for the performing arts (Yale).

# Abbey Theatre
# Staff & Supporters

An Roinn Ealaíon, Oidhreachta,
Gnóthaí Réigiúnacha, Tuaithe agus Gaeltachta

Department of Arts, Heritage,
Regional, Rural and Gaeltacht Affairs

The Abbey Theatre gratefully acknowledges the financial support of the Arts Council of Ireland and the support of the Department of Arts, Heritage, Regional, Rural and Gaeltacht Affairs.

Archive partner of the Abbey Theatre.

# 2016 Abbey Theatre Supporters

# Donegal

Frank McGuinness was born in Buncrana, Co. Donegal, and now lives in Dublin and lectures in English at University College Dublin. His plays include *The Factory Girls* (1982), *Baglady* (1985), *Observe the Sons of Ulster Marching Towards the Somme* (1985), *Innocence* (1986), *Carthaginians* (1988), *Mary and Lizzie* (1989), *The Bread Man* (1991), *Someone Who'll Watch Over Me* (1992), *The Bird Sanctuary* (1994), *Mutabilitie* (1997), *Dolly West's Kitchen* (1999), *Gates of Gold* (2002), *Speaking Like Magpies* (2005), *There Came a Gypsy Riding* (2007), *Greta Garbo Came to Donegal* (2010), *The Match Box* (2012) and *The Hanging Gardens* (2013) Among his many widely staged versions are *Rosmersholm* (1987), *Peer Gynt* (1988), *Hedda Gabler* (1994), *A Doll's House* (1997), *The Lady from the Sea* (2008), *Oedipus* (2008), *Helen* (2009), *Ghosts* (2010), *John Gabriel Borkman* (2010), *Damned by Despair* (2012) and *The Dead* (2012).

Kevin Doherty was born in Buncrana, Co. Donegal, and now lives in Dublin. He has played music professionally since the age of nineteen. He is a member of the traditional band Four Men and a Dog and has recorded six albums with them, most recently *And the Band Played On*, to mark twenty-five years together. Kevin recorded three solo albums and one album with the band Telegraph. He is currently working with them on their second album, due out in the autumn. His songs have been recorded by Levon Helm, Rick Danko and Mary Black. Kevin provided the music for the film *Watermelon* (Blinder Films).

*also by Frank McGuinness*

GATES OF GOLD
DOLLY WEST'S KITCHEN
MARY AND LIZZIE
SOMEONE WHO'LL WATCH OVER ME
MUTABILITIE
OBSERVE THE SONS OF ULSTER MARCHING TOWARDS THE SOMME
SPEAKING LIKE MAGPIES
THERE CAME A GYPSY RIDING
GRETA GARBO CAME TO DONEGAL
THE MATCH BOX
THE HANGING GARDENS

FRANK McGUINNESS PLAYS ONE
(*The Factory Girls,*
*Observe the Sons of Ulster Marching Towards the Somme,*
*Innocence, Carthaginians, Baglady*)

FRANK McGUINNESS PLAYS TWO
(*Mary and Lizzie, Someone Who'll Watch Over Me,*
*Dolly West's Kitchen, The Bird Sanctuary*)

*translations and adaptations*
A DOLL'S HOUSE (Ibsen)
PEER GYNT (Ibsen)
ELECTRA (Sophocles)
OEDIPUS (Sophocles)
THE STORM (Ostrovsky)
HECUBA (Euripides)
MISS JULIE (Strindberg)
PHAEDRA (Racine)
THE LADY FROM THE SEA (Ibsen)
HELEN (Euripides)
DAMNED BY DESPAIR (Tirso de Molina)
THE DEAD (Joyce)

*screenplays*
Brian Friel's DANCING AT LUGHNASA

THE DAZZLING DARK: NEW IRISH PLAYS
(edited by Frank McGuinness)

# FRANK McGUINNESS

# Donegal

*Music by Kevin Doherty*

FABER & FABER

First published in 2016
by Faber and Faber Limited
74–77 Great Russell Street
London WC1B 3DA

Typeset by Country Setting, Kingsdown, Kent CT14 8ES
Printed in England by CPI Bookmarque, Croydon, Surrey

A CIP record for this book
is available from the British Library

978–0–571–33575–6

2 4 6 8 10 9 7 5 3 1

For Celine and Selena
Always

**Donegal** was first performed at the Abbey Theatre, Dublin, on 6 October 2016. The cast, in alphabetical order, was as follows:

**Magdalene Carolan**  Deirdre Donnelly
**Jackie Day**  Killian Donnelly
**Hugo Day**  John Kavanagh
**Conor Day**  Frank Laverty
**Irene Day**  Siobhan McCarthy
**Liam Brogan**  Keith McErlean
**Triona Brogan**  Ruth McGill
**Joanne Carolan**  Eleanor Methven
**Liza Field**  Megan Riordan

*Musicians, in alphabetical order*

Paul Brennan  *pedal steel/banjo/guitar*
James Delaney  *band leader/keyboards/accordion*
Jason Duffy  *drums/percussion*
Kenneth Edge  *alto saxophone/clarinet*
Jack Maher  *bass/guitar*
Conor O'Farrell-Brady  *guitar*

*Director*  Conall Morrison
*Musical Director and Arranger*  Conor Linehan
*Set Designer*  Liam Doona
*Costume Designer*  Joan O'Clery
*Lighting Designer*  Ben Ormerod
*Sound Designer*  Alexis Nealon
*Audio Visual Designer*  Arnim Friess
*Movement Director*  Muirne Bloomer

# Characters

**Irene Day**
a singer

**Conor Day**
her husband

**Jackie Day**
her son

**Triona Brogan**
her daughter

**Liam Brogan**
her husband

**Hugo Day**
Conor's father

**Magdalene Carolan**
Irene's mother

**Joanne Carolan**
Irene's sister

**Liza Field**
an American visitor

*Time*
Now

*Place*
Donegal

# Locations

SCENE ONE        *Outside*
SEENE TWO        *Inside/outside*
SEENE THREE      *Outside*
SCENE FOUR       *Inside*
SCENE FIVE       *Outside*
SEENE SIX        *Outside/inside*
SCENE SEVEN      *Inside*

## Production Notes

*Donegal* is a play with songs.

The set should be sufficiently flexible to reflect that crossing of boundaries between speech and music.

The production can decide where outside and inside meet and divide.

The landscape and house, its furniture, its contents, even its very construction, are of this county: elemental, volatile, changeable.

These are a deeply restless people. They rarely sit, and, when confined, even then they are plotting or at war.

The staging of the songs at the top of and within each scene, and the nature and number of musicians – these are of the production's choice.

*This play script went to press before the end of rehearsals, so will not reflect any late changes to dialogue or music.*

# DONEGAL

# PROLOGUE

*Irene sings 'At My Mother's Grave'.*

**Irene**
I held my mother's hands
Leaving Donegal.
I kissed my mother's head
Leaving Donegal.
Those safe hands held me tight
Leaving Donegal,
As I wandered the earth
Leaving Donegal.

Today I took my stand
At my mother's grave.
Today my eyes turned red
At my mother's grave.
I wept the dark night through
At my mother's grave.
At my mother's grave.

I hold my mother's hands
No matter where I stand.
I kiss my mother's head
And let my eyes turn red.
Her fingers hold me tight
Through every sleepless night
As I wander through the earth
Mourning the one who gave me birth.

I held my mother's hand
Leaving Donegal.

I kissed my mother's head
Leaving Donegal.
Those safe hands held me tight
Leaving Donegal,
As I wandered the earth
Leaving Donegal.
As I wandered the earth
Leaving Donegal.

## SCENE ONE

**Magdalene**  We made a terrible mistake. Chronic.

*Silence.*

Aren't you going to ask me what it was?

**Hugo**  I'm not, no.

**Magdalene**  Why so stand-offish?

**Hugo**  Give my head peace. You'll come out with some gibberish I'm tired hearing.

**Magdalene**  All I was going to say, if pressed to it, we should never, ever as a species have taken the first steps on to land out of the ocean. We should have stayed as fish.

**Hugo**  Why?

**Magdalene**  Gills. Nicer looking than lungs. And you couldn't smoke with them boys. We'd have saved a fortune on cigarettes. The whole human race – all the world over. The Russians, fierce smokers – the Chinese never without a butt behind their ears – Yanks, don't talk to me. Not one of them would have lit up if we'd stuck to the water. Think of the money wasted. There might never have been wars. That's as true as I'm sitting here. It's also why I can't stomach plaice. It would be like eating my own. And me being afflicted with this connection to fish, is it any wonder my daughter is an old trout? What did your son ever see in her? Maybe it was what he heard. Hasn't she got a lovely singing voice?

17

**Hugo** No.

**Magdalene** I beg to differ, and so do many others. Miss Irene Day, Ireland's queen of country, or easy listening, or crooning – or whatever under Jesus she calls it. I could never stick her, but who am I to argue?

**Hugo** He puts up with her, he does – my son, Conor.

**Magdalene** Why wouldn't he? Irene's proved herself to be a prize catch. A fine pair of gills belting out all the crowd's favourites. I would love to give you a blast of one – something typical she might sing, but I can't, for I remember not one. All forgettable – instantly forgettable, that's how I would describe my daughter's repertoire.

**Hugo** Have you ever had a good word to say about her?

**Magdalene** Now, now, there's one thing I can blow my own trumpet about – I've never let rip to her face, it's only behind her back I destroy her. Two-faced perhaps, but perfectly capable of playing the kind mother.

**Hugo** It must be an awful struggle.

**Magdalene** Don't you know it is? Don't you know it's why I've barely spoken to the bad bitch in years – the effort to either say something nice or say nothing? Isn't it why she gets into a panic on occasions thinking I've lost my powers of speech?

**Hugo** She knows you have your powers of speech – you're plonked in their house, my son's and herself's, guzzling their grub and drinking –

**Magdalene** Like a fish? How could I not be? Weren't we all, as I said, from the ocean –

**Hugo** So, you're some class of human halibut? She knows full well you can speak.

*Silence.*

That's not going to work.

*Silence.*

You need not think clamming up because I challenge you will work.

*Silence.*

I don't care how long this silence lasts, you can stew –

*He goes to leave.*

**Magdalene** God forgive you for abandoning me – I've had a stroke.

**Hugo** You've not had a stroke.

**Magdalene** I may as well have for all the attention I get from them, my own. I may as well be lying under the clay.

**Hugo** When you do, I'll organise the ceilidh. They'll be turning up in droves.

**Magdalene** Shut it – she's coming –

**Hugo** The enemy?

**Magdalene** Now, back me up in all.

*Irene enters.*

**Irene** You two lovebirds in cahoots as always? Great to be courting morning, noon and night. Can't wait till you name the big day and you finally get hitched. Can you give us a clue how soon so I can save for a hat?

**Magdalene** The hospital.

**Irene** What about a hospital?

**Magdalene** An ambulance.

**Irene** Do you follow her?

**Magdalene** Doctors and nurses.

**Irene** Where is she at?

**Magdalene** Typhoid – diphtheria – angina – diabetes.

**Hugo** I'm teaching her to keep track of the names of diseases.

**Irene** She doesn't suffer from any.

**Hugo** Not to the best of our knowledge, but it's always good to be prepared. And isn't it great she has such a grip on her vocabulary?

**Irene** She's in no danger of losing it, is she? Why do people fall for the shenanigans of this wicked woman? Don't tell me you believe them – I know you don't. Siding with her just delays the day when chickens come home to roost and one of you is stricken with a serious illness –

**Magdalene** Sing a wee song about it – make us all cry.

**Irene** You heard that – you heard her. She's compos mentis enough to mock me. You're my witness, Hugo, to her badness. Mock on, Mother – mock with the rest of them my wee songs. Just let me inform you the same songs have for many years paid to keep you at ease, clean and comfortable, waited on hand and foot by us and all I employ –

**Hugo** You employ one skitteny housekeeper – your sister.

**Irene** It's more than most people can. And it's her who sends me out here on this mission to inquire what you and my thundering bitch of a mother will deign to eat for your dinner.

**Hugo** Should I ask her? I'm not sure she'll follow me. She has moments of great confusion.

**Irene** My fist might rid her confusion –

20

*Magdalene whines, frightened.*

**Hugo** Talk like that scares her.

**Irene** I'm so sorry – I meant to give her a choice. Would she prefer my boot?

**Hugo** Enough of your old buck, my lady. Your poor mother –

*He takes Magdalene's hand as she whimpers.*

There, there, Magdalene. Irene doesn't mean anything. She's only joking. She likes making fun, as she calls it, or as others call it, taking a hand at the old and sick. She wants to know about your dinner – what would you like to eat?

**Magdalene** A big pair of men's drawers. Clean.

**Hugo** Bacon and cabbage. That means she'd love a mouthful of bacon and cabbage if it's going.

**Irene** A pair of drawers she's asked for – a pair of drawers she'll get. Don't say I don't spoil her.

*She exits.*

**Hugo** God help us all, but do you know what I'm going to tell you?

**Magdalene** She spoils me?

**Hugo** She does, you know.

**Magdalene** Indeed. I wish I didn't hate her.

**Hugo** How long have you hated her?

**Magdalene** Too long to remember it starting. Since I was in my fifties? No – maybe it was my forties. A long, long time, but to our credit it's lasted fresh as a daisy all these years. We're loyal in our loathing if nothing else.

**Hugo**  Why do you loathe her?

**Magdalene**  She annoys me profoundly. They all do. Jesus, I look at them and ask, did this shower in some way or form all spring unaided out of my unfortunate loins? If they did, those same loins have plenty to answer for. Why are they all sniffing around this house anyway? Is it Christmas or some other godforsaken gathering?

**Hugo**  You know rightly it's not Christmas.

**Magdalene**  Ding-dong merrily in hell. Don't say it's Easter – eggs turn my stomach. Even chocolate ones.

**Hugo**  It's not Easter. Guess –

**Magdalene**  I stopped guessing when Donegal won the All-Ireland Football Final. It was the end of chance – or maybe the end of luck, who could say.

**Hugo**  Guess –

**Magdalene**  I'm not guessing –

**Hugo**  It's your birthday.

*Silence.*

**Magdalene**  Why are they allowed do this to me? What age am I?

**Hugo**  Nobody's allowed to say.

**Magdalene**  No, they're not – and don't you let them forget it. Wait a minute – I was born the beginning of October – the year's nowhere near that. It's not my birthday.

**Hugo**  Just testing.

*They both burst out laughing.*

**Magdalene**  Do you think I riled Irene, do you?

**Hugo**  I'd say we did.

**Magdalene**  She knows that I know she knows?

**Hugo**  I'd say she does, but I don't know what you know
she –

**Magdalene**  She's a right little show-off, isn't she?
Warbling for Ireland.

> *To Hugo's merriment, Magdalene mimics Irene's 'At
> My Mother's Grave': 'At my mother's grave / Grieving
> for Donegal / Lough Swilly and Lough Foyle'.*

> *Fade.*

<br>

### SCENE TWO

*Jackie and the company sing 'Feasting on Herring'.*

**Jackie**

Feasting on freshest, feasting on herring
I wandered the streets of old Amsterdam
I felt northern seas in my two palms.
What did that city of diamonds bring
To my eyes and ears but a shine of herring?

My Amsterdam lover gazed in my eyes
Whispered, sweet darling, tell me no lies
Have you walked the streets of my city before,
City of diamonds and delicate whores,
Feasting on freshness, feasting on herring. (*Three times.*)

Dance with me, on the banks of canals,
Dance with your lover, let cities fall,
Swim with me in teeming shoals,
Where sagas are told, where sagas are told.

I woke with a start in my lover's bed,
My pockets were empty, my heart turned to lead,

While shepherds are shearing, their flocks standing shorn,
Where is my lover this fair morn?
Feasting on freshness, feasting on herring, (*Three times.*)

Dance with me, on the banks of canals,
Dance with your lover, let cities fall,
Swim with me in teeming shoals,
Where sagas are told, where sagas are told,
Feasting on freshness, feasting on herring. (*Five times.*)


*A buffet brunch/barbecue.*
*The whole family help themselves to food and drink.*
*Triona busies herself at the buffet table.*
*Joanne quietly, efficiently, quietly goes about her work.*

**Triona** All hands – now, tuck in. Don't be shy. It's a pleasure to feed you.

**Liam** You aren't feeding them. Your mother bought what we're eating.

**Triona** Thank you for being so kind to tell me – even more kind for making sure everyone else can as well. Now, as I was saying before I was rudely interrupted –

**Liam** What was rude about it?

**Triona** Tuck in – don't be shy.

**Liza** We won't be. What a spread.

**Triona** Isn't it beautiful?

**Liam** Self-praise is no praise.

**Liza** Salads in Ireland – they're so green. God, what a geeky thing to say.

*Triona hands Liam a plate of food. She whispers.*

**Triona** If you don't shut your mouth, pal, you won't be eating this – you'll be wearing it.

*Liam takes the food.*

**Liam** I hope it won't choke me.

**Triona** If it should, then it does us all a favour. Father, can I get you a plate of something?

**Conor** I'll hold my horses.

*He turns to Liza.*

That daughter of mine will have us all fat as fools.

**Liam** I weigh the same as I did the day I married Triona.

**Conor** Did I say different?

**Liam** Why the sneer about me being fat?

**Irene** Who was sneering? You're the only one with a face on him.

**Liza** I mean it – I sure do. A splendid spread.

**Liam** I suppose you would expect twice this amount in front of you if you were in the States. I spent a summer there as a student. The waste of food was shocking. Don't get me wrong, Liza. Better a feast than a famine always. And they're very generous – Yanks. But they just don't have a notion where to stop.

**Irene** You must have felt at home then.

**Liam** Not really – no. I watch every bite I put into my mouth. I have to –

**Liza** In case you do put on a few inches –

**Liam** No – in case my wife does poison me. She often threatens.

**Irene** She's not the only one, Liam.

**Triona** I might be doing it even as we speak. Been doing it for years maybe. Some of these toxins take time to kick in. Bit by bit, morsel by morsel, drip by deadly drip – carrying you to the coffin and churchyard, me getting away scot free.

**Conor** Many's a woman done it before.

**Irene** Many's a woman's doing it now.

**Triona** Many's a woman will do it again.

*She cackles.*

**Liam** That's lovely, that is. I'm terrified now to swallow a bite. You shower would see me dead – what harm did I ever do you but marry Triona?

**Irene** Will you catch yourself on, boy? Will you not take your medication?

**Triona** Let him rant – who's listening?

**Irene** (*sotto*) Make him take his pills.

**Triona** (*sotto*) He thinks he doesn't need to. Give me time.

**Conor** You might be a happier man, Liam, if you could learn to take a joke.

**Liam** So life's a joke, is it, Conor Day? I'm surrounded by you and your gang of comedians breaking their sides laughing at who? Me – isn't it always me? What did you do for a laugh before I arrived to entertain you?

*He points to Irene.*

Listen to her crowing for the country her ancient laments? The whole nation mocks them. Surely she's made her fortune out of them, but haven't they left her a laughing stock? Doesn't her own son ridicule her in his music –

**Joanne**  Do we have enough eggs?

*Silence.*

Should I cook more eggs?

*Silence.*

**Irene**  Do you, Jackie?

**Jackie**  Do I? No.

**Irene**  Ridicule me – do you?

**Jackie**  What do you want me to say? I said no –

**Irene**  Still, I should listen to the musical achievements of my son and heir.

**Triona**  I'm sure he is –

**Liza**  Have you never heard his songs? That's hard to believe –

**Irene**  Isn't it? But then I have dear diehard fans like my pleasant son-in-law ready to repeat all that needs spewing in my direction from certain quarters, that certain quarter being you, Jackie, in case you're wondering.

**Conor**  Let things lie for a while at least – Jackie's just in the door.

**Irene**  And we're all glad to welcome him back from the US of A. Even more glad to welcome you, Liza. Aren't you, Conor? The last occasion our brilliant genius of a son graced us with his presence he brought home his boyfriend.

**Liza**  Yes, I know – it was my brother, Stuart. I doubt if they were really lovers. Were you, Jackie?

**Jackie**  How would I know?

**Liza**  Well, you're not now. We met at Stuart's wedding –

**Conor** I can't keep up with this. Who was he marrying – a horse?

**Liza** No, another guy.

**Conor** Thank God my father and your mother are not here to witness –

**Irene** That piece of work – her? My mother? What are you talking about? She'd be in her element at any contrary act. Did you say you were cooking more eggs, Joanne? Then do so – stop standing with your mouth open listening to your betters' business.

**Joanne** There's nobody here my betters.

**Irene** Who pays you?

**Joanne** You might do so, but that doesn't entitle you to fling abuse.

**Conor** I hardly think she was doing that.

**Joanne** What entitles her to look down her long nose –

**Conor** Again, I say she wasn't –

**Joanne** You stick up for her –

**Conor** She is my wife –

**Joanne** She is my sister – you picked her –

**Irene** You say it, and I stand –

**Joanne** When you're sober enough and not sprawling –

**Irene** Are you implying I have a drink problem –

**Joanne** Implying nothing – Declaring you'd lick drink off a dead Christian Brother's leg.

*Liam claps his hand in glee.*

**Liam** Oh slap it into them – slap it into them.

*Silence. Both sisters look at Liam.*

**Joanne** Slap it into us, yes, Liam?

**Irene** Who's going to do the slapping?

**Joanne** Would it be yourself, Liam?

**Irene** Would you raise your hand against us?

**Joanne** Like Father, like yourself then, Liam?

**Irene** The way your father broke your mother's jaw.

**Liam** Stop.

**Joanne** The way he strapped you, Liam.

**Irene** Strapped you – stripped you – left you naked on the street.

**Liam** Make them stop, Triona.

**Joanne** We'll stop – but with this warning.

**Irene** Don't push your luck, Liam.

**Joanne** It might lead you where you don't want to go.

**Irene** Were you talking about making eggs, Joanne?

**Joanne** I was, but I've gone off the idea.

**Irene** Maybe Liam hasn't – ask him.

**Joanne** Would you fancy more eggs, Liam?

*He shakes his head.*

**Irene** Runny – nice and runny – run – Liam – run, nice and runny.

*Liam charges out of the room.*

**Triona** I know he needed dealing with, but you two are some pair. I could have got him back on his tablets without this. Well, maybe I couldn't. But you might have given me a chance.

*She goes after Liam.*

**Liza** I think he deserved that.

**Irene** Did you? Why? Are you trying to fit in here?

**Jackie** Why do you think I brought her home?

**Joanne** Tell us why, Jackie. Tell you Aunt Joanne. Haven't we no secrets? What's the fun and games this time? Forgive me – I'm talking as if you weren't there, Liza –

**Liza** I'm there all right. We're here because we want to be. Working together. Writing new songs. Letting them come as they should come. Loads of songs. All inspired by here – by Donegal. Maybe even a whole album we could make together –

**Jackie** Man and wife –

**Joanne** Man and wife – wife and man –

**Jackie** Me and her –

**Conor** You and her –

**Jackie** We might get married –

**Irene** On the rebound. From her brother. Charming. I'm told you had to be peeled off him some nights down at the hotel –

**Jackie** We booked separate rooms. All very proper. I wouldn't offend my mother. What would people in the town say? And now look at me. A creature transformed –

**Irene** Are you?

**Jackie** You know what men are like, Ma. Changeable creatures. Want you one minute, dump you the next.

**Irene** I wouldn't know.

**Jackie** What would you say, Da?

**Conor** You've lost me there, mister.

**Irene** Grist to the mill, isn't this, Jackie? Land home – spring a surprise – Last time, I'm a queer – this time, I'm not. No, I bring home a blushing bride-to-be, and she doesn't have a cock. Or maybe she does. Is that the next revelation?

**Jackie** Why would I do that?

**Irene** Ammunition.

**Jackie** Against you?

**Irene** Yourself. Against yourself. Cause chaos. Watch the reaction – note it down – write songs. Sing them. You all over. You never change, son. I have always and ever been able to read you like –

**Jackie** A book? You've never read one –

**Irene** Correction. I have never finished one. There was no need. I knew who did it, halfway through. Why waste time wondering when you know what's what?

**Jackie** Nothing could shock you – you knew it all, just like your music?

**Irene** You were once glad to sing it –

**Jackie** A long time ago.

**Liza** He still sings the songs you taught him.

**Conor** I did my bit as well.

**Jackie** Then you're both the guilty party.

**Joanne** Our grandfather started him. He learned him 'The Shoals of Herring'. The family song. Once upon a time our lads were all fishermen. Jesus, had we not some courage then?

**Irene** We still do.

**Joanne** When we cross the road now, we bless ourselves – cowards.

**Jackie** He didn't teach it to me.

**Irene** What?

**Jackie** 'The Shoals of Herring'. I learned it from a record. My da's record.

**Joanne** But he sang it – my father – all the time – your grandfather –

**Jackie** Who's fighting that he sang it? I'm saying –

**Joanne** It was my father taught you –

**Jackie** I heard it on a record –

**Joanne** But it's in your bones – in your blood – from our side, not his, not your da –

**Liza** It's just a song. Who cares?

**Joanne** I care, for it's more than that. It's our anthem –

**Liza** There's a million anthems. Can I have some coffee?

*She helps herself to coffee.*

**Joanne** Tell her, Irene – 'Shoals of Herring' – it's our family's –

**Irene** It's your fantasy – how you want to remember our father.

**Joanne** That song is our story, we lived it –

**Conor** She'll be claiming next she wrote it –

**Joanne** It must have been some family connection to us –

**Liza** A man called Ewan MacColl wrote it.

**Joanne** That's a lie – he lifted it from my father – I swear to that –

**Liza** He did write it, MacColl.

**Joanne** Fetch me my mother.

**Liza** Jack, stand up for me. You know who wrote 'Shoals of Herring'.

**Joanne** My mother will be my witness.

**Liza** Come on, Jack – speak up –

**Joanne** Fetch her, Conor.

*Conor exits as Jackie takes Joanne's hand.*

**Liza** Ewan MacColl –

**Jackie** Maybe he didn't.

**Liza** What?

**Jackie** She'll settle this – my grandmother. I want to hear what she says.

**Irene** Jackie, this is pure badness on your part keeping this up. Stop him, Conor – make him stop. Where's Conor?

**Joanne** Gone to fetch my mother. They're here.

*Conor, Magdalene and Hugo enter, followed shortly by Liam and Triona, as Jackie releases Joanne's hand.*

Here they are, now she'll answer –

**Magdalene** Answer what?

**Joanne** 'The Shoals of Herring', that song –

**Magdalene** I can't say I know it.

**Joanne** Of course you do –

**Magdalene**  Don't sing it to me. You have no voice.

**Joanne**  But you must remember how it goes.

**Magdalene**  Is it about drowning?

**Irene**  About fishing – fishing for herring, as you well know.

**Magdalene**  For a lot of men in this county – Donegal – that's the same as drowning.

**Liam**  There she's speaking the truth.

**Magdalene**  Poor chaps sent out in murderous weather to search for fish, left to gasp their last breath. The ocean cared as little for them as the bastards who reaped what profit was waiting in waves sweeping men from wives and children, thrown against the mercy of the cruel Atlantic. Do I remember some soft snatch of music that insults the lives of lads hardy enough to risk all to scrape a living out of the water? You wonder about who wrote a song? I say, wonder on. I wouldn't wipe my arse with it.

**Hugo**  She doesn't know it so – 'The Shoals of Herring'.

**Magdalene**  Get me out of here. I'm poisoned looking at them. They all think they're lovely. Well, you're not. My two daughters, you look ancient – older than I do. Where's my grandson?

*Jackie salutes.*

**Jackie**  Present and correct, Grandma.

**Magdalene**  In my day 'Granny' was good enough, what's with this 'Grandma'?

**Joanne**  That's telling him.

**Magdalene**  Did I ask for your intervention?

**Joanne**  You didn't.

**Magdalene** Then stick your snout out of the trough. Young fella –

**Jackie** What?

*She points to Hugo.*

**Magdalene** Fred Astaire is not as nimble on his pins as he once was. I've had enough of this trevally, get me out, I want a word with you.

**Irene** What about?

**Magdalene** What is it in this house, people to a man or woman cannot mind their own bloody business? What is it to you what we have to talk about, me and him? Do we need permission –

**Irene** I thought it might be to do with his wedding. You were going to stretch your hand into your shroud and pay for it. Oh, of course, you weren't here when he announced his intentions. He's getting married soon –

**Magdalene** To whom?

**Conor** This girl – the Yankee.

**Triona** Jesus, he's joking. Jackie's pulled some fast ones in his time, but this beats Banaghher. He has got to be joking.

**Liza** Thank you for the kind welcome.

**Liam** It's as best as you'll receive, get used to it if you're considering you might enter the fray in this establishment. Hang around and I'll show you the scars I've had inflicted.

**Triona** Not from me.

**Liam** Did I say they were from you? You don't marry one woman or man in this clique, you end up with the lot of them, and each is as big a rip as the other.

**Magdalene** So you're tying the knot?

*She points to Liza.*

And this is the lucky lady? Which of you will be wearing white? No, not her. Not you, pet, eh? I'd advise something beige – with a large scarlet 'A' pinned to your arse. Isn't that what you excel at? I hope it is, to match your husband's taste. Hugo, I changed my mind. You – remove me. Forget the blushing couple. They must have a million things to discuss about the happy day when God smiles on their union.

**Hugo** Do you think I move like Fred Astaire?

**Magdalene** Only if he drove a tractor.

*Hugo and Magdalene are gone.*

**Liza** Isn't she –

*Silence.*

Hasn't she –

**Irene** Her own way of going, or as I call her, Caligula.

**Liza** I like her.

**Liam** You have no rivals.

**Triona** She's yours for the taking.

**Liza** They'd love her in the States, Jack.

**Conor** In the middle of the Mohave Desert.

**Liza** She'd die there.

**Liam** Don't bank on it.

**Liza** Poor Grandma.

**Jackie** It's 'Granny', we say Granny here.

**Liza** Granny then – sorry.

**Joanne**  What point?

**Liza**  Sorry?

**Conor**  Being sorry – what point? That's what she meant, wasn't it, Joanne?

**Joanne**  I never know what people mean, Conor.

**Irene**  I hate to end this engrossing confab, but we'll soon have to hit the road if we're to make Monaghan in good time.

**Triona**  Are you back tonight?

**Irene**  I plan to be – the days of staying in hotels are gone.

**Joanne**  Will I go with you for company?

**Irene**  What would you be doing sitting getting your death in a frozen marquee?

**Triona**  I might come along as well – give you a hand. I can talk to Auntie Joanne while you're singing. Let me go –

**Irene**  I have your father with me. Ask your father.

**Triona**  Do you want us along, Da?

**Conor**  Who's stopping you?

**Joanne**  So you have no objections?

**Conor**  More the merrier.

**Irene**  Maybe one of you might stay and cast an eye over the bar and restaurant –

**Triona**  Very few in during the middle of the week. They can run themselves –

**Irene**  They can't, you know.

**Triona**  What do you pay your manager to do?

**Joanne** Give Triona that wage and she'll jump to it, but she can't be expected, no more than myself, to do another's job. We can call a halt to this –

**Conor** Why?

**Joanne** Irene seems not too keen.

**Irene** Come as you like – I hope you find plenty to entertain yourselves.

**Joanne** Sure we can listen to you.

**Irene** I know how much delight you take in my singing voice –

**Joanne** You never know, I might be converted. I'm off to get ready.

*She exits.*

**Triona** I'll travel as I am.

**Liam** Is there dinner in the fridge?

**Triona** Fish fingers, remains of last night's baked beans in a bowl beside them, a box of matches to light the gas should the ignition fail, that's you fed. Amn't I the lucky woman, hitched to a man so easily pleased?

**Liam** Just as well I am.

**Conor** Liam, if there's one thing you're not, it's easily pleased. Get a move on, all coming on the road with us. I want to make a best fist of the distance before it's dark.

**Irene** Are the boys already on the road?

**Conor** The band will be there an hour or so before we arrive.

**Irene** That hour or so worries me. Does it mean they might not be entirely sober?

**Conor**  On the money you shell out to them, can they afford booze?

**Irene**  You see they get a fair share of our cash.

**Conor**  And that's why they stay with you, best in the business, as befits the Queen of Country in the Emerald Isle, Miss Irene Day –

**Irene**  Less of the blather, I've heard it before, slugging around the country, frozen to the marrow, changing my tights in one dirty kip after another – I could do a guided tour of every ladies' lavatory in Ireland. How in hell have I not caught typhoid?

**Conor**  That's showbiz, missus, you know that –

**Jackie**  They bleed you dry.

*Silence.*

In this house. They all do.

**Irene**  But you don't, Jackie boy. You don't need to. Raking in a fair few shillings stateside I hear whispered. Too wise to tell how much. Too tight to hand over something in return for his rearing. Mean with money –

**Jackie**  What stone did I lick that from?

**Irene**  Your da – who else? From me you get your beauty and your sunny disposition. While we're out tonight, talk to your granny. She's been counting the days and hours till you got here. She might not show it, but she's dying about you. Humour her, have a conversation.

*Irene and Conor exit, followed by Triona, who calls back to Jackie.*

**Triona**  Do as she says, Jackie – the old one is dying about you, they all are.

**Liza**  Dying about you – what an Irish way to love each other.

*She goes to embrace Jackie. He lets her, looks at her and then leaves her alone. Fade.*

### SCENE THREE

*Song, 'Ladies In Waiting', sung by Liza, Triona and Jackie.*

**Liza**
  I work for my living
  By serving in bars.
  Men ask for the moon,
  I give them the stars
  And in return
  For some nickels and dimes
  I thank them kindly
  And speak of old times.

**Liza / Triona**
  I should be at church
  Mending my soul,
  The Lord knows I let
  My life turn too cold,
  I should be at home
  Lighting a fire
  Not listening to tales
  Of broken-heart liars.

**Liza / Triona / Jackie**
  They salute the ladies in waiting,
  Raise a glass to ladies in waiting,
  Good luck and cheers
  Good health and more beers.
  Serve us, ladies in waiting.

**Jackie**

    She stands and she looks
    In the bar's lengthy mirror,
    Her face is as faded
    As the blonde of her hair.
    If she could fly
    On a flying trapeze,
    She would grow wings –
    The honey bee's knees.
    Her dress it is black
    As the sky in the night,
    And she is an orb
    That can catch the light.
    Like moths to a flame,
    The men gather round,
    Out of their mouths
    They pour these sweet sounds –

**Chorus**

    We salute the ladies in waiting,
    Raise a glass to ladies in waiting,
    Good luck and cheers,
    Good health and more beers,
    Serve us, ladies in waiting.

*Outside, evening.*
    *The remainder of a child's abandoned playground.*
*A broken seesaw.*
    *A rattly swing.*
    *One small weathered set of goalposts, nearly toppled*
*on to the ground.*
    *Hugo pushes Liza gently on the swing.*
    *Liam watches.*

**Liam** If we do have children, I would like them, boys or
girls, to have Russian names – Yuri and Ilya, or Natasha
and Tamara.

**Liza** You've been to Russia? You know the language?

**Liam** Not a word, nor have I set foot there. When I was at school, I had a pen-pal – she lived in Minsk. I always dreamt after Gorbachev she might come to Donegal, but no show. Got her exams, I suppose. That was that with her letters.

**Liza** And you still carry a torch –

**Liam** Jesus, don't let Triona hear that. I don't, of course. I never set eyes on her apart from one tiny photograph in black and white she sent as a thank you for a Christmas present I posted to her. Talcum powder, called Apple Blossom. She never wrote afterwards. It has nothing to do with her that if I had a family, I'd call them for Russian saints. There are saints in Russia?

**Liza** There must be – The magnificent icons –

**Liam** There's another reason for naming them so –

**Hugo** He wants you to ask the reason.

**Liam** Let her ask if she wants to know. I'll tell her anyroad. You see, I maintain in the next thirty years, who'll rule the world? Russia. Why? Desperate times are coming. Who'll thrive best? People who've survived all this earth can throw at them.

**Liza** What about the Chinese?

**Liam** I'm not saddling any kid of mine with a name that foreign. They'd have the lining kicked out of them at school. I'll stick by the Russians – here's why. They outlasted Hitler, they buried Stalin, they're taking more and more control of the West, and they'll thrive in global warming – they themselves have all sorts of weather, so they know how to cope. Nothing frazzles them. When they invade Ireland – and they will – for our fertile soils –

they'll meet my youngsters and fall on top of them,
delighted to find any connection. Hence the names – 'Are
you grand, Yuri' – 'Shake my hand, Ilya' – 'Give us a
kiss, Tamara' – 'How are you doing, Natasha?' You see
how we're on the winning wicket?

**Liza** No – I don't, I'm afraid.

**Liam** That's a pity, but sure who cares? I don't have any
wains anyway. How long are you staying?

**Liza** That's up to Jack.

**Liam** We call him Jackie.

**Liza** Jackie is really a girl's name in America.

**Liam** Well, it's not here.

**Hugo** Jackie Kennedy, of course. And Bobby. Why oh
why did he have to die? Why, Bobby Kennedy, why?
There was a song with that in it. Did Irene sing it? Can't
recall. It didn't explain why he died, the song. He was a
brave man, Bobby, and you're a very brave girl.

**Liza** Am I?

**Hugo** A very courageous young lady, if I may say so –
Liza, isn't it?

**Liza** Well, I try to be brave, so thank you – Hugo, isn't it?

**Hugo** How else would you manage to live there –
America? A savage place, lawless altogether. I would
never set foot in it. Look what happened to a poor soul
born not that far from here. Wasn't she the unfortunate
won the holiday of a lifetime in New York, all expenses
paid? We all know what occurred, God bless us and
save us.

**Liam** Didn't the papers call her Mary from Dungloe?

43

**Hugo** Her name was Mary, she came indeed from Dungloe, and she was brought back to it in a box.

**Liza** She died?

**Hugo** She was shot – by a doughnut. That's as true as I'm standing here.

*Liza leaves the swing. Hugo sits on it.*

**Liam** What makes you believe she was shot by a doughnut?

**Hugo** They're not like ours – a bit of jam and sugar sprinkled on it. No, they stick a whole menagerie of stuff into theirs – a three-course dinner in one doughnut. What do you think was in this tragic woman's? A bullet. She took it as a raisin or piece of chocolate. Swallowed it whole into her stomach. Went off inside her. Her organs flew everywhere – kidneys, lungs, pancreas, spleen. She hadn't a chance. The blood was brutal. And, here's the killer, lads. She had just made her first holy communion. At the age of thirty-six.

**Liza** I dread to ask this, but why did she wait to be thirty-six –

**Hugo** Marriage. She was on her honeymoon after getting married. To a Catholic. She was Church of Ireland. She'd taken her time converting. They're great like that, Protestants, when they turn. They want to know everything about the sacraments. That's why when you do get them to the altar rails, eventually you have to beat them away, or Mass would last till the cows come home. Some of the more blackhearted among her own tribe whispered she got what was coming to her. Aren't people capable of being very cruel?

*Magdalene and Jackie enter.*

44

**Magdalene** What are you doing on that swing? Have you gone back to the wain's wit?

*Hugo continues swinging.*

Have you lost your power of hearing as well as your reason? Are you listening to me? What will you be up to next? Swallowing chewing gum and eating ice-pops?

*She puts to Jackie.*

You see, young fella, that's what happens to you when you don't speak. You turn into your boyo Hugo here, God bless the mark.

**Hugo** What do you mean, God bless the mark?

**Magdalene** He's recovered. He talks. It's a miracle. And it would take a miracle again to get more than two words out of my grandson. When did you grow so silent?

**Jackie** I answered what you asked me.

**Magdalene** Not much joy in that, not much of a surprise.

**Liza** What kind of surprise would you like?

**Magdalene** Rather than answering that, could I ask you a question? You, like my grandson, are a class of singer – now I'm sure you're tired hearing this, but I have to find out what puzzles everyone –

**Liza** How I remember all the words to songs?

**Magdalene** No. I was hoping you could tell me, if in a quadrangle all sides are equal, what's the square root of the largest angle? You can give it to the nearest prime number. Can you enlighten me?

**Liza** Sorry – I can't.

**Magdalene** So you're shite at maths then – you had to turn to the music? Did you pass any other exam? I'd say if you did, it was by the skin of your big teeth.

45

**Liza** The compliments are flying.

**Magdalene** Better they than fists. I asked why you're so silent, boy – answer it, you, not your trollop.

**Liza** I beg your pardon – trollop, you call me?

**Magdalene** Madam, your week's washing wouldn't be overloaded –

**Liza** What does she mean?

**Liam** Ignore her. She was never the same since she spent a night in Limavady.

**Liza** What's a Limavady?

**Hugo** You're not the first to ask that –

**Liam** And you won't be the last –

**Hugo** And everyone a sorry woman.

**Magdalene** Excuse me, I think Limavady is beautiful.

*Magdalene, Liam and Hugo laugh hysterically, even Jackie joining in.*

We can laugh and Christ forgive us mocking, but we could all end up living there.

**Jackie** Limavady?

**Magdalene** Might be all we can afford. Maybe I've spoken out of turn, have I, Liam?

**Liam** How would I know – Who tells me anything?

**Magdalene** I'm in the same boat – they say nothing or next to it to the old fool shooting her mouth off. You're just in the door, Jackie. They won't be landing you with the shock we'll soon have to get out of the house. The funds aren't there. The restaurant – the bar – they're emptying. No one has money. This country these past few

46

years, we've taken a terrible battering. We're no exception, are we? Did they say we might be facing ruination?

*Jackie shakes his head.*

Still can't rouse a sound out of him.

**Liam** Maybe he's not that concerned.

**Hugo** Why would he not be?

**Liam** Maybe he's making plenty of money singing himself.

**Hugo** Maybe he'll put his hand in his pocket.

**Liam** Bail out the mother and father.

**Hugo** Save his family.

**Liam** If he can, he will.

**Hugo** But he's a quiet fellow, modest, my grandson, he'll say nothing till he has to.

**Magdalene** I think he'll do nothing.

**Liza** Why not?

**Magdalene** Eaten bread is soon forgotten. Once upon a time, the feasts we had in this house.

**Jackie** Open another bottle.

**Magdalene** People forget.

**Hugo** Children forget.

**Jackie** Carve another chicken.

**Hugo** Have the men enough Guinness?

**Liam** Let the Bushmills flow.

**Magdalene** Eat till you can eat no more.

**Jackie** My generous father.

**Hugo** Always too generous –

**Magdalene** And Jackie, give us a song.

**Jackie** No, let my mother sing – she's not that keen on me competing –

**Magdalene** She's not here to stop you. Sing one I taught you. Sing, Jackie.

*Jackie sings 'The Minstrel Boy'.*

**Jackie**
The Minstrel Boy to the war is gone
In the ranks of death you will find him;
His father's sword he hath girded on,
And his wild harp slung behind him;
'Land of Song!' said the warrior bard,
'Tho' all the world betrays thee,
One sword, at least, thy rights shall guard,
One faithful harp shall praise thee!'

*Liam, Hugo and Magdalene join in chorus for the second verse.*

**Chorus**
The Minstrel fell! But the foeman's chain
Could not bring that proud soul under;
The harp he lov'd ne'er spoke again,
For he tore its chords asunder;
And said, 'No chains shall sully thee,
Thou soul of love and brav'ry!
Thy songs were made for the pure and free,
They shall never sound in slavery!'

*There is silence at the song's end.*

**Hugo** Don't see us put on the street, Jackie.

**Liza** I really shouldn't be in this conversation.

**Liam**  You tell him to fork out – you can do that –

**Liza**  Why would he listen to me?

**Liam**  He declares he's going to marry you.

**Liza**  How would I know how much money he has?

**Magdalene**  It must be a pretty penny – why else would you marry him?

**Liza**  Aren't you the sharp one?

**Magdalene**  Or maybe it's you who's loaded?

**Liza**  You're as nasty an old dear as I've ever trodded upon. You're so full of it, lady, maybe Jack doesn't talk to you because he's tired shovelling all your crap behind you. Maybe he's stopped speaking your language. I haven't. What I have to say is, old girl, you smell.

**Magdalene**  You'll survive. You'll last the pace. Jackie, do something for this delightful girl.

**Jackie**  What?

**Magdalene**  Slap her – slap her hard in the big mouth.

**Liza**  That would be the last thing he ever does.

**Magdalene**  Get me inside – we need more words.

**Liza**  Me?

*Magdalene points at Liam and Hugo.*

**Magdalene**  I'm not talking to the dead, am I? Move yourself.

*Liza goes to take Magdalene out.*

As far as I'm concerned, you have two things going for you. You don't play the spoons, and you're not called Fiona.

*Liza and Magdalene exit.*

49

**Liam** Your mother, will she let you tie the knot?

**Jackie** How bad are things?

**Hugo** On the money front?

**Liam** They're bearing up.

**Hugo** They're sinking.

**Liam** The restaurant's holding its own.

**Hugo** On its knees. And her music, your mother, Irene –

**Liam** Not the draw she was.

**Hugo** Less people want to hear her. But they'd pay to listen to you. Don't say I said that. Say we said nothing.

**Liam** We're not supposed to know.

**Jackie** Am I?

**Hugo** Nobody is.

**Jackie** How's he faring – my father?

**Liam** Right as rain. Conor Day. Not a bother. Serene –

**Hugo** That's us – serene – serenity itself, the Days. Different to the Carolans, your mother's breed.

**Jackie** What he doesn't want to see, he's blind. He's deaf to what he won't hear. He has her as bad.

**Liam** Are you going to save them?

**Jackie** Are they going to ask me? No, never. What can I do then?

**Hugo** That's for you to tell us. We should mend that see-saw.

**Liam** Why? Broken for years – no babies growing up to use it.

**Hugo**  Who knows when they soon might be? You and Triona, never lose hope.

**Liam**  I don't, Hugo.

**Hugo**  If you say so, Liam.

**Jackie**  Hope – sweet hope.

**Liam**  It's been years since I had a go on a swing. Would anybody mind –

**Hugo**  Fire away.

> *Liam sits on the swing. Hugo pushes him.*
> *They cry out 'Wheee' in unison.*
> *Jackie looks at them and then leaves.*
> *Hugo continues to push Liam on the swing.*

> *Fade.*


### SCENE FOUR

*Irene, Liza and Triona sing.*

**Irene**
> The man in the moon
> Looks into your eyes,
> Sleep sleep sleep child.
>
> Birds of the air from
> Paradise,
> Sleep sleep child.
>
> The man in the moon
> Looks into your eyes,
> Sleep sleep sleep child.
>
> Birds of the air from
> Paradise,
> Sleep sleep sleep child.

*Irene, Liza, Triona and Liam sing in Chorus.*

**Chorus**
The man in the moon
Looks into your eyes,
Sleep sleep sleep child.

Birds of the air from
Paradise,
Sleep sleep sleep child.

The man in the moon
Looks into your eyes,
Sleep sleep sleep child.

Birds of the air from
Paradise,
Sleep sleep sleep child.

*Liam and Triona sing in duet.*

**Duet**
The man in the moon
Looks into your eyes,
Sleep sleep sleep child

The birds of the air
From Paradise
Sleep sleep child.

*Triona sings alone.*

**Triona**
The man in the moon
Looked into your eyes,
Sleep sleep sleeping child.

The birds of the air
From Paradise
Sleep sleep sleeping child.

*Inside.*
  *Night.*
  *Liam sits on his own beneath a small lamp.*
  *He sleeps, waiting for Irene, Conor, Triona and Joanne*
*to return.*
  *Hugo sits somewhere in the darkness of the room.*
  *Unseen, he can be heard whispering.*

**Hugo**  Are you awake, Liam? They're very late back,
aren't they?

  *Silence.*

I should not wake Magdalene though – she'd be like a
bear. But maybe she can't shut her eyes – she's awake too –
What do you think?

  *Silence.*

Liam, are you awake? They're very late back, aren't they?

  *A car is heard driving up, its lights illuminating the
  room.*

They're home.

  *The car stops.*

They're safe, I hope. Are you awake, Liam?

**Liam**  How in Jesus could I not be, listening to you
hissing like a snake in the dark?

  *He switches on a light.*
  *Hugo busies himself, hidden, in a large armchair,
  facing the wall. Triona is first to enter, switching on
  more lights.*

**Triona**  Did you miss me?

**Liam**  How did the night go?

**Triona**  Herself in fine voice.

**Liam** She always loves Monaghan.

**Triona** Monaghan always loves her.

**Liam** The roads to there now, would you know them?

**Triona** So much better than before. Now there's no bother across the border, they're safe as houses –

**Liam** Fly down, fly back.

**Triona** Two hours – just over – the journey home – no fear of being stopped –

**Liam** Changed times – it would have once taken –

**Triona** Best part of three – on the road I always think of the Miami Showband – massacred, God rest them – years ago –

*She starts to prepare drinks.*

**Liam** Did they have a big feed organised for you all? Did you stay around –

**Triona** For a drink? No.

**Liam** She just wanted to get on the road –

**Triona** Wanted home, yes.

**Liam** Were there many at it?

**Triona** The show? A fair few.

**Liam** Irene was content?

**Triona** When is she ever? What did you do with yourself?

**Liam** Just stayed up.

**Triona** Granny in bed?

**Liam** As far as I know.

**Triona** Hugo see her upstairs?

**Liam** Is he not there to ask him?

**Triona** Can't spy him.

**Liam** Then he must have hit the hay.

**Triona** Our American friends?

**Liam** Jackie and Liza went for a meal – have a taste of how the restaurant's faring. Maybe they went for a nightcap to the bar afterwards.

**Triona** So we can expect them back?

**Liam** I'd say so.

**Triona** I hope they go straight to their beds. Anything for a quiet life.

**Liam** Irene's in fighting form?

**Triona** Not her, exactly.

**Liam** Surely not your father –

**Triona** How would it be him – come easy, go easy, as always. No, it's the aunt.

**Liam** Joanne? Under the weather? Drunk as a skunk?

**Triona** Shunkish.

**Liam** She can hold plenty though.

**Triona** When she puts her mind to it.

**Liam** Many at the show?

**Triona** You asked me that already. I answered. What did you want me to have done? Count them? Who's coming now? Just you keep your lips sealed. I said nothing about how the night went.

**Liam** Well, you didn't.

**Triona** That's a good start.

*Irene and Joanne enter. Irene is still in her glamorous, glittering stage costume with an abundance of silver everywhere.*

**Irene** Joanne, why did you let me get into this rig-out? Look at the amount of silver. It's like cooking foil, and me the turkey wrapped in it. Were it Christmas time, I'd be nervous.

*She collapses on a sofa, kicking off her high heels.*

I am here, thanks be to Jesus. Thanks be to his parents, Mary and St Joseph, I am back. I am home, thanks be to the sweet and gentle and most divine fuck.

*Triona hands Irene a drink.*

Oh pet, you are worth your weight in gold for having this ready – my first of the night, my darling child.

*Triona hands Joanne a drink.*

**Joanne** It's not mine.

*Silence.*

What's with the dirty look? Have I grown two heads?

**Triona** Look in the mirror – you'll probably see double.

**Joanne** I'm the one said what had to be said – what you should have spoken out if you'd been looking out for your mother, my sister. That Monaghan gang have some nerve.

**Irene** I asked you in the car to give this matter a rest, Joanne. Now we're in the house, I ask you once more. Could you be so kind as to do what I tell you? Remember this is all my business, not yours, not Triona's, not anybody else's.

**Triona** I did not stick my oar in.

**Joanne** But you should have.

**Irene** I said, shut it. Just shut it.

*She nearly shouts the last 'Shut it'. The intensity shocks them all, including Irene.*

That came out louder than I intended. Apologies.

**Joanne** No need for you to apologise, Irene.

**Triona** Auntie Joanne's right. You need say sorry to no one.

**Liam** What happened?

*Silence.*

Can you not say?

*Without warning, Irene suddenly starts singing 'Phil the Fluter's Ball'.*

**Irene**
Have you heard of Phil the fluter from the town of
    Ballymuck?
The times were going hard for him, in fact the man
    was broke.
So, he just sent out some notices to his neighbours
    one and all,
As to how he'd like their company that evening at
    a ball.
When writin' out he was careful to suggest to them,
That if they found a hat of his convenient to the door,
The more they put in whenever he requested them,
The better would the music be for batterin' the floor.

*Irene grabs Joanne into the song.*

**Irene / Joanne**
With a toot on the flute and a twiddle on the fiddle-o!
Hopping in the middle like a herrin' on the griddle-o!

Up! Down! Hands around! Crossing to the wall!
Oh, hadn't we the gaiety at Phil the fluter's ball.
All joined in with the greatest joviality,
Covering the buckle, and the shuffle, and the cut;
Jigs were danced of the very finest quality,
The widow be't the company at handling the foot.

**Triona** We loved Mam singing that as children.

*She grabs a reluctant Liam into the performance and
joins up with Irene and Joanne. Conor enters and is
also hauled in as they sing in Chorus.*

**Chorus**
With a toot on the flute and a twiddle on the fiddle-o!
Hopping in the middle like a herrin' on the griddle-o!
Up! Down! Hands around! Crossing to the wall!
Oh, hadn't we the gaiety at Phil the fluter's ball.

*At the conclusion, Irene falls into Conor's arms.*

**Conor** Jesus, it doesn't take much for you to get a second
wind.

**Irene** No, it doesn't, but then, isn't that my life, Conor,
coasting by on second winds – would you not say so?
You as well, Joanne? Get your father a wee drink, Triona.

**Triona** I am a dutiful daughter – I've already done so.

**Irene** And replenish me.

**Triona** Ma, your diabetes –

**Irene** This is the point when I should say, it won't kill
me – you should all shout back, yes, it will. Prove it –
pour.

*Triona does so – a large one.*

**Irene** You can't kill a good one – and I never was. Make
of that what you will. How long would you give me to
live anyroad?

**Joanne** It's too early in the night for her to grow morbid –

**Irene** Five years – four – three – two – one – gone – Will you cry for me?

**Triona** Buckets –

**Liam** Oceans –

**Irene** Conor, what about you?

**Conor** My eyes out – cry my eyes out –

**Irene** Then you'll be blind – you can get blindness from diabetes, you know –

**Joanne** You can get fucking everything from diabetes – stop looking for sympathy.

**Irene** Is that what I do? Or is that your job, Joanne? Looking for sympathy for this old horse here?

**Joanne** I would whip the same old horse –

**Irene** Was that not why you started your shouting after the show tonight?

**Joanne** I got upset for you – that's all.

**Irene** Why were you upset?

**Joanne** I'm saying nothing.

**Irene** You had plenty to say earlier.

**Joanne** I just thought you were owed an apology.

**Irene** If I were, I would have asked for one – not you.

**Joanne** Excuse me for butting in – I won't in future. But if Conor was going to keep his mouth closed –

**Conor** Why drag me –

**Joanne** Because it was your wife that was insulted –

**Irene** I was not insulted.

**Joanne** How many people paid to see you tonight? Less than a hundred.

**Irene** Thanks for counting.

**Triona** There were more than that.

**Joanne** Seventy-seven.

**Irene** My lucky number.

**Joanne** The takings won't pay for petrol there and back.

**Irene** What's that to you?

**Joanne** I'm thinking only of you and Conor –

**Irene** Then stop thinking.

**Joanne** This cannot go on. Losing money, hand over fist. It costs you more to work –

**Conor** You'll still be paid your wages –

**Joanne** It's not my wages I'm after. Not them I worry about. It's my sister. Her reputation. How long has this woman been at the top of the ladder? For enough years to deserve better than singing to a near empty tent? Why is that? Because nobody knows she's there. Not a bean spent on advertising her, too mean to do more than hand her a cup of cold tea after two hours on that stage.

**Irene** They don't want to come.

**Triona** Ma, that's not true – if they knew you were there –

**Irene** They would still stay away in droves.

**Triona** I cannot believe that – why would they?

**Irene** Will you tell her, Conor, or will I?

*Silence.*

Up to me then. Triona, I am what's politely called in my business 'past it'. Not the draw she used to be, I believe they now say. The crowd's moved on to another gallows. They've voted with their big feet. We've missed the chase. The boot has been put in. Have it what way you like, but we're kaput, my dear – finished.

**Liam** Never say that. You'll wish it on yourself.

**Irene** It's already been wished on me.

**Liam** But you're the best in the country.

**Conor** The country's moved on.

**Irene** It's left me behind.

**Liam** Why are you lying down and taking it? Why aren't you fighting –

**Conor** What in hell do you think she's been doing these past five years?

**Joanne** These past thirty years for her, since she was barely in her teens – singing her guts out – trailing from one miserable town to another – every fair county in Ireland – no other woman for company, only a bunch of young fellas, barely the privacy to wash her underwear or get a decent bite of food – selling that first record. How proud we were, Irene. You must remember.

*Irene sings her first hit, 'The West's Awake'.*

**Irene**
 When all beside a vigil keep,
 The West's asleep, the West's asleep –
 Alas! And well may Erin weep
 When Connacht lies in slumber deep.
 There lake and plain smile fair and free,

61

'Mid rocks their guardian chivalry.
Sing, Oh! let man learn liberty
From crashing wind and lashing sea.

That chainless wave and lovely land
Freedom and nationhood demand;
Be sure the great God never planned
For slumb'ring slaves a home so grand.
And long a brave and haughty race
Honoured and sentinelled the place.
Sing, Oh! not even their sons' disgrace
Can quite destroy their glory's trace.

And if, when all a vigil keep,
The West's asleep! the West's asleep!
Alas! and well may Erin weep
That Connacht lies in slumber deep.
But, hark! a voice like thunder spake,
The West's awake! the West's awake!
Sing, Oh! hurrah! let England quake,
We'll watch till death for Erin's sake.
We'll watch till death for Erin's sake.

**Liam** Still stirs the blood, Irene.

**Conor** The voice of Ireland – said it then, say it now.

**Irene** And no one wants to hear it, darling. We all know times change. My voice is old hat. My music's down the Swanee, down the Shannon, down the Swilly – take your pick. Who do they want to hear now?

*Liza and Jackie enter.*

**Liza** We're back.

**Irene** That's who they want to hear. My son, and his like. Are you with her, Jackie? Are you home as well?

**Jackie** Safe and sound.

**Irene** Glad to hear it.

**Jackie** How did tonight do?

**Conor** Great.

**Triona** Brilliant.

**Joanne** You should have been there.

**Liza** I would have loved to –

**Irene** But you weren't there, and neither was he – and nobody minds, so no apologies. Did you enjoy your meal?

**Liza** It's a nice restaurant –

**Joanne** No, it's not – we can't get cooking staff to stay, and the waiters and waitresses are from these parts, so they've manners that match our own. You won't be rushing back, would you? Was there more than yourself eating?

**Liza** Not when we arrived. Then word got out Jack was there, we barely got a chance to taste the food – and yes, it was pretty awful – but so many people called in –

**Conor** Did they order meals?

**Liza** No, they just wanted to talk to Jack –

**Conor** Did they at least have a few drinks?

**Liza** They just wanted to shake his hand.

**Conor** Wanting to know people's business.

**Jackie** Spot on, Father.

**Liza** I thought they were friendly.

**Jackie** Do you know who were friendliest?

**Irene** The ones who mocked you most when they had the chance.

**Jackie** Don't worry, Ma – I know. Would you like the litany of names?

**Irene** Spare us that.

**Jackie** They still jeer at me without mercy, but now it happens behind my back, and do you know what – maybe America's made me soft, but I prefer it that way.

**Liam** Nobody jeers at you any more, Jackie.

**Jackie** You'd stop them, would you, Liam?

**Liam** Yes, I would –

**Triona** And he would as well. You always have the hateful habit of running your own down. It's getting worse, it really is. All right, you had to venture to America to get a bit of notice – run away from under Ma's shadow –

**Jackie** Was that why I went?

**Conor** How would you describe it?

**Jackie** Stop being my mother's son – try to live it down –

**Irene** Well, there you have it – in a nutshell. That's what I fight against. And who's my worst enemy? My son and heir –

**Liza** Whose music you won't listen to –

**Irene** Why should I do him that favour if all he does with mine is scorn it?

**Liza** Have you really never heard a single song he's written?

**Irene** I might have stepped in one without noticing –

**Conor** Jesus, that's a bit of an ancient one –

**Irene** I'm sorry to offend with old jokes, but what can you expect? I'm well behind the times in all respects, don't you know that?

**Liza** I still think you might apologise –

*Jackie bursts out laughing.*

I mean it, Jackie – She should say sorry –

**Triona** Sorry is not a word my mother often uses. Correction, uses ever.

**Conor** The shock of saying it would kill her.

**Irene** This lady would beg to differ – this lady thinks I should be on my knees –

**Liza** I didn't go as far as that –

**Irene** I heard you – we all did.

**Liza** Why do you keep pushing things so far –

**Joanne** So now she's pushy?

**Conor** Thanks be to Christ she has been – just as well for all of us –

**Liza** Yes, I think she goes beyond pushy. She's a ballbreaker.

*Silence.*

You heard me. Ballbreaker. And Jack hasn't let her do that to him. That's what really annoys her about him.

**Irene** What do you say to that, my darling son? Am I what she says? Are you terrified to answer? Should you be?

**Liza** He won't say –

**Triona** Why not?

**Liza** Because he knows you. All about you. All you did wrong. He knows you failed.

**Irene** As a mother? As a singer? Failed?

*Silence.*

You stay silent, Jackie.

**Conor** He'll defend you.

**Irene** I don't think he will.

**Triona** He better.

**Irene** No better about it. He believes she's right. It's not what she's said shocks him. It's when. Why the haste to accuse? Why has so careful a lady got her timing so wrong? What's gone awry? Oh, I've got it. She's still not at all sure about him. She's a bit nervous – maybe more than a bit. He's not quite deflowered you yet, has he? You've been let keep the old maidenhead intact for once. But then you've lost it before in a thousand rides, haven't you, old flower?

*Liza laughs and applauds Irene.*

**Liza** Wow, I'd say if you could still summon half of that spirit on stage you'd still be selling tickets.

**Conor** She sells enough.

**Liza** That's cool, Conor – defend her.

**Joanne** Why should he not?

**Liza** That's not for a stranger to say.

**Triona** I've had enough.

**Liam** You've upset Triona, Jackie.

**Triona** How dare you attack my innocent mother and father? How dare you bring such a woman into our home?

66

I would throw the pack of you into the street if this were my house –

**Jackie** It will be yours, Triona, you know that –

**Triona** I do not. Stop this –

**Liam** You're upsetting Triona, you always do.

**Jackie** Makes a change from you doing it. My being here brings some respite –

**Triona** I do not need respite –

**Jackie** You nurse him – that's all you do – all you expect to do, and every woman in this place, they do precisely the same – nurse men.

**Conor** Then what do you suggest women should do with men – shoot them?

**Jackie** Put them down – no, only one deserved that fate. Me – better to have put that boyo down at birth. Remember?

**Irene** Remember what? I never raised a hand against you.

**Jackie** No need, when you can spit poison –

**Joanne** Everyone says things in temper they don't mean –

**Jackie** You weren't in temper, Irene, were you? Better I had not been born –

**Conor** She was depressed –

**Jackie** Better for her, better for you –

**Conor** It was depression, she needed minding –

**Joanne** You sent her out to work –

**Conor** It was what she wanted –

**Jackie** Morning, noon, and night.

**Conor** That's what they advised, doctors then.

**Jackie** What you advised.

**Conor** She wanted to get out of the house. Get away from – from –

*Silence.*

**Jackie** Her daughter? No.

**Triona** She never made any difference –

**Jackie** Between us? She made a difference.

**Joanne** Long memory.

**Jackie** Time to let it go, would you say?

**Irene** That's down to you. Our American friend will hinder that –

**Jackie** No, she's helped. To forgive – forgive my mother. Do you want to hear how?

*He sings 'Broken Glass Slippers'.*

Well I know a man who fell in love
With a woman, two hands in one glove –
With rings on her fingers and bells on her toes,
Having music wherever she goes,

And I know a woman who fell in love
With a man, two hands in one glove –
With rings on their fingers and bells on their toes,
Having music wherever they go,
Put on their feet, bare stockinged feet,
Boots that could stamp on naked feet,
Boots that could shatter delicate glass,
Delicate glass, slippers of glass.
Slippers of glass.
Slippers of glass.

And I know of lovers when love had died
They asked their children to take sides.
Well tell me whose love you care to choose,
Tell me, I'll give you delicate shoes,
Put on their feet, their fragile bound feet,
My babies with fast bounded feet,
Slippers of glass, broken sharp glass,
Broken sharp glass, slippers of glass.
Slippers of glass, slippers of glass.

*As he sings the last verse, Triona, Liam and Joanne leave.*

I know a father who loved a mother,
I know a mother who loved a father,
Rings on their fingers and bells on their toes,
Making music as love comes and goes,
Put on their feet, their bare stockinged feet,
Boots that could stamp on naked feet,
Boots that could shatter delicate glass
Delicate broken slippers of glass.
Slippers of glass. Slippers of glass.
Slippers of glass. Slippers of glass.

*There is a silence when he finishes, broken by Irene.*

**Irene** That is not me. That is not my life.

**Conor** That's what you think of us?

**Irene** You know nothing about my life. Nothing.

*Irene and Conor leave Jackie and Liza.*

**Liza** It's her, isn't it?

**Jackie** She says not. What she says goes.

**Liza** They're you, aren't they – you and Triona, delicate broken slippers –

**Jackie** If the shoe fits –

*He sings.*

**Jackie**
Put on my feet, bare stockinged feet,
Boots that could stamp on stockinged feet,
Boots that could shatter delicate glass,
Broken sharp glass, slippers of glass,
Delicate broken slippers of glass.

**Liza** Yes, the shoe fits.

**Jackie** Maybe. And she listened to the end at least. Who knows? It might save her. Save her house, I mean. Good night.

*He starts to exit, humming, 'I told you I came out at night, / To kiss, to dance in the green light.'*

**Liza** Wait – I'll go up with you.

**Jackie** If you like.

*They exit, and Hugo emerges from the darkness.*

**Hugo** I wonder what will I tell Magdalene? Should I say anything? Will she be delighted to hear how they're battling? Will she be charmed they're killing each other?

*He exits.*

*Fade.*

## SCENE FIVE

*Music, electric guitar solo. Jackie sings 'The Green Light'.*

**Jackie**
I took your life into my hands.
I drove you past the breaking point.
I left you stranded in bad lands,
And swore that I would wreck this joint,
If you don't give me what I want,
If you don't give me what I need,
What I need and what I want,
If you don't give, if you don't give,
If you don't shine, and bite,
I'm waiting for the light,
Oh I'm waiting, I'm waiting for the light.
Green light, I'm waiting, waiting.

Who was it took me for a ride?
Who said my heart is as good as gold?
Who looked aside when I cried?
Who shot the breeze? The sun turned cold.
You chanced your luck, you chanced it twice.
I told you you would pay the price.
You told me to come out at night,
When it was safe to see the light,
Safe to kiss, to kiss, kiss beneath the light,
Oh save the dance and kiss beneath the light.
Green light. I'm waiting.

We held our breath, we jumped for joy,
We shook the clock, we turned it back,
We called each other girl and boy,

We gave each other what we lacked,
We changed our luck – we changed it twice,
You told me we would pay the price,
I told you I come out at night,
I told you I come out at night,
When it is safe, safe to shine,
Safe to shine in the light.
Shining in the light.
Oh. Safe to dance and kiss beneath the light.
Green light I'm waiting, waiting for the light.
Oh. I'm waiting. I'm waiting for the light.
Green light.  I'm waiting, I'm waiting for the light.


*Outside. Morning.*
*Joanne wheels Magdalene.*

**Magdalene**  So there was a bit of a barney then?

**Joanne**  I've heard tell there was.

**Magdalene**  Any blows struck?

**Joanne**  Your guess is as good as mine, Mother.

**Magdalene**  But you were there.

**Joanne**  In body, yes, but maybe not in spirit. I differ in that respect from your best buddy, the bold Hugo, whom I didn't see there, but as you're so well informed, I have no doubt he conveyed all the necessary. Quit pestering me for more details.

**Magdalene**  It's always the details he forgets are the juiciest, and do you know why he forgets them?

**Joanne**  To madden you?

**Magdalene**  He cannot now and never could tell a story. Everything arsewise, time and place, who said what, where and when – useless, not a notion, all well and good if it's only gossip you're after, but if you're seeking for a little more, then accuracy is everything.

**Joanne** What more do you want than gossip?

**Magdalene** Assassination. I like my stories to have the killer touch. The wee detail that proves to be fatal – that leaves them gasping as if drawing their last breath, the punch in the solar plexus, the knife between the shoulder blade, the hat pin through the eyeball.

**Joanne** You know you were wasted here as a bad bastard –

**Magdalene** I know – I should have gone into the Church. But the glass ceiling – what woman in her right mind would settle for sister or reverend mother?

**Joanne** You fancied yourself a bishop?

**Magdalene** Bishop, my hole – for me, it was Pope or nothing. Beautiful residence in Rome, best of pictures on your wall, gorgeous vestments, white and yellow, always my colours, and best of all being carried everywhere in a chair, with the weather roasting every day. A great life, but not for the likes of me, or you if it comes to it. Tits, bloody tits, Catholics hate them. Red flags to a bull. Red. 'Red rover, red rover, I call Joanne over.' Do you recall playing that as a child?

**Joanne** No.

**Magdalene** Just came into my head – I can't say why. This happens more and more often. Going back to being a child. Myself, you, Irene, Triona, and the boy. Jack – Jackie, I hear he accused her of hating him. Did he? No need to answer. She did, you know. She might have done him damage. Lost her reason a bit.

**Joanne** It was not as bad as that.

73

**Magdalene**  It was worse. I had to rear him.

**Joanne**  Mother, now that is a confounded lie. We all did our bit. Conor, as well, he was an excellent father for the time it was, attentive –

**Magdalene**  Wouldn't pay for a nurse. Wouldn't hear of it. That's the man all over. He would not spend money on his dinner if he thought he could leg it and not be caught.

**Joanne**  Maybe he's had his fingers badly burned in the past.

**Magdalene**  Or maybe behind all that hail fellow well met, he is as miserable a drink of water as ever walked from here to Dublin to save a bus fare.

**Joanne**  After all these years, what now have you got against your son-in-law?

**Magdalene**  He married the wrong daughter.

*Silence.*

He landed the wrong sister. Do you think I don't know that? Do you not know it?

*Silence.*

You've hid it well, all three of you. No one would suspect a thing. You'd need to have eyes like a hawk to notice. Eyes in the back of your head. And I have, Joanne. Your poor heart, daughter. It must have been broken so many times. Or nearly broken, and that's worse.

*Silence.*

I've spoken out of turn.

**Joanne**  Sorry, were you speaking? I must have dozed off. I didn't hear a word. Were you being intimate? That must be why I switched off. When you get personal, you always

74

mistake me for Irene, and in that confusion you say things I shouldn't hear. That's why I let such talk pass merrily over my head.

**Magdalene** That's me put in my place. I'm only doing my best –

**Joanne** That's the hideous thing – you do think it's for the best, but what pleasure can you get setting us on each other? Do you know what delight we take in defying you? All your efforts to drive me and Irene apart, yet we still care enough about your old carcass to keep from committing you – why do we bother?

**Magdalene** Lovely language – carcass indeed.

**Joanne** Accept my sincere regrets, Mother. How can I make it up to you? Have you ever been skiing?

**Magdalene** You know rightly I haven't.

**Joanne** You just put your feet in the air and go, wheee.

**Magdalene** There's cuts and concussion –

**Joanne** You'd break every bone in your body. It would save me doing that to you. Then you're a goner –

**Magdalene** I'm not at my end yet, lady.

**Joanne** You're as near as makes no difference.

**Magdalene** None of us knows the day or hour we're called.

**Joanne** Know this for certain – you will be called before I am. And don't expect to be buried.

**Magdalene** You'd begrudge me a coffin?

**Joanne** Why need one if you're being dumped over a pier? You'll get a wheelbarrow and a black plastic bag. I'll pay for all from the onions I'll sell.

**Magdalene** Onions?

**Joanne** Shifting like hot cakes as we drown the corpse. Cut and put raw red to the eye, nobody would shed a tear willingly.

**Magdalene** Am I not the pity of a woman? And you threaten me with the home –

**Joanne** Money's tight in every corner.

**Magdalene** Irene would never do that to me. Conor wouldn't let her.

**Joanne** You're safe on your perch here. The cash isn't there to put you into the lap of luxury of a home.

**Magdalene** You haven't seen many if you think they're luxury.

**Joanne** Yes, I have. Quite a few. Not that long ago. Irene and myself, we decided best be prepared. If we have to commit you one day, we should have some idea where to leave you lying. A few acceptable establishments round here. Quite nice. Did we not tell you?

    *Silence.*

Must have clean forgotten. Now, it was myself and Irene, we did the tour, didn't we? Maybe it was myself and Conor – aren't we married? Or is it just as you declare, we should be?

    *Silence.*

I'm all at sea – you have me completely mixed up. Aren't you the desperate woman being so mistaken?

    *Silence.*

I'm sorry – did I say the wrong thing? I'm only doing my best.

*Magdalene starts crying.*
  *Joanne loses her temper.*

What the hell are you blabbing for?

*Magdalene continues crying. Joanne tries to calm her.*

Stop this – stop –

**Magdalene** I'm scared to death of going into such a place. Why do you torture me by threatening this? I don't have a witness to prove you did, but I heard you. Why do you frighten me so much?

**Joanne** Mother, I will never put you in there.

**Magdalene** Then promise me – promise to good God.

**Joanne** I promise.

**Magdalene** To good God –

**Joanne** To good God, I promise.

*She pats Magdalene's hair.*

**Magdalene** Am I the worst mammy in the world?

**Joanne** Yes.

**Magdalene** Worse than your sister?

**Joanne** In her way, she is worse –

**Magdalene** Will he save her? Jackie?

**Joanne** Why should he?

**Magdalene** Will he save us? Has he the money to bail us out?

**Joanne** So it's said.

**Magdalene** Is he worth a fortune already?

**Joanne** That's what his father believes.

**Magdalene** Conor's an awful boaster.

**Joanne** Let's hope he's not in this case.

**Magdalene** Have him and Jackie spoken?

**Joanne** Not to my knowledge.

**Magdalene** So it's all in the clouds.

**Joanne** Up in the clouds.

**Magdalene** I see them coming. Triona, her useless lump of a man, and the American Jackie's threatening to saddle himself with – isn't she a dose? What's she called?

**Joanne** Liza.

**Magdalene** She's dangerous.

**Joanne** How?

**Magdalene** She could get to know too much. I'd have to silence her.

**Joanne** What with?

**Magdalene** A harpoon. Very effective. My father had one. Did a bit of whaling in the States. I swear to good Christ he could wield that weapon as if it were a toothbrush. Not that he'd thank you for thinking him womanish, cleaning his teeth. Where is it now, the harpoon? I hear you ask. Like everything else, disposed of – somewhere in a skip. These people, I want to avoid them. Get me away.

**Joanne** They're nearly on top of us – hold your ground, say hello.

*Triona, Liam and Liza enter.*

**Triona** Granny, just the woman we want.

**Magdalene** Why?

**Triona**  Because you can tell us what we need to know.

**Magdalene**  I'm useless to you – I forget everything. I've done it deliberately – lost my memory.

**Triona**  Granny, God forgive you.

**Magdalene**  Entirely up to him, but I've packed it in, remembering things. Waste of effort. Only causes bother. Far better off letting others do it for you. Whatever you want to know of me, make it up. More reliable in the long run. Or at least you're more likely to believe it.

*She turns to Liza.*

Why are you looking at me as if you'd devour me?
Do you mind if I ask why so many of you Yanks have gorgeous teeth? Is it from never going hungry?

**Liza**  There are plenty folk in America short of food –

**Magdalene**  The ones who troop here, I've never heard their guts rattling – yet they'd still take the hand off you if you gave them a ham sandwich. Maybe you're the exception. Has anybody seen this specimen eating? I might have done so, but as I said at the start of this conversation, I forget everything – so that's my excuse. What were you looking to know?

**Triona**  Why bother asking if you've no answer?

**Magdalene**  Who says I haven't?

**Triona**  You do.

**Magdalene**  Aren't you great the way you heed me when you shouldn't? Ask.

**Triona**  Did my mother ever top the Irish charts?

**Joanne**  She did – a fair few years ago.

**Triona**  Which song?

79

**Magdalene** Some old twaddle about a kip in Antrim no sane man or woman would set foot in if given a chance to be well clear of it.

**Liam** Carrickfergus, didn't I tell you? Irene was one of the first – if not the first – to make it well known. I learned it off her record.

*Liam sings 'Carrickfergus'. Triona joins in and, more tentatively, so does Liza in the third verse.*

**Liam**
I wish I was in Carrickfergus,
Only for nights in Ballygrant.
I would swim over the deepest ocean, the deepest ocean
For my love to find,
But the sea is wide and I cannot cross over
And neither have I the wings to fly.
I wish I could meet a handsome boatman
To ferry me over, to my love and die.

My childhood days bring back sad reflections
Of happy times I spent so long ago,
My boyhood friends and my own relations
Have all passed on now like melting snow.
But I'll spend my days in endless roaming,
Soft is the grass, my bed is free.
Ah, to be back now in Carrickfergus,
On that long road down to the sea.

But in Kilkenny, it is reported,
On marble stones there as black as ink
With gold and silver I would support her,
But I'll sing no more now till I get a drink.
For I'm drunk today, and I'm seldom sober,
A handsome rover from town to town,
Ah, but I'm sick now, my days are numbered,
Come all you young men and lay me down.

**Joanne** It sold by the lorry-load – very popular on both sides of the religious divide, that number.

**Magdalene** It didn't take off in the town itself – people in Carrickfergus were too miserable to buy a single copy.

**Triona** You know the song, 'Carrickfergus'?

**Liza** Jack sings it – it's a favourite – I've heard him often –

**Liam** He couldn't – he never would.

**Liza** Why wouldn't he?

**Liam** That's his mother's song. That's my song. He wouldn't steal it, he's no thief –

**Magdalene** Get me out – get me away –

*Joanne does so.*
  *Magdalene turns to Liam as she leaves.*

Thief – my grandson? He'd take the bite out of your mouth. I should know, I reared him. How do you think our breed survived this hungry county? Me and him, are we not the same?

*Magdalene and Joanne exit.*

**Liza** You sang the song so beautifully – I really didn't mean to upset you.

**Liam** Think nothing of it – it's just, 'Carrickfergus', that's special, very much so. I never sing it in public out of respect for Irene, and I thought – Jackie, he might not out of respect for me – he might keep his dirty hands off it if he had any manners. Wouldn't you think he might restrain himself, Triona?

**Triona** Liam and Jackie, when they were small –

**Liam** Don't say we were pals, we were not –

**Triona**  I know well you weren't –

**Liam**  Nobody would sit willingly with him at school, or play –

**Triona**  That's not what –

**Liam**  I might have occasionally, out of pity, and I never called him cissy.

**Triona**  All I wanted to say was that at one time Liam had the better voice.

**Liam**  His own sister says it, not me.

**Liza**  What happened?

**Liam**  My voice? It broke.

**Liza**  All boys' voices break. Didn't Jack's?

**Liam**  His came back. Stronger than ever.

**Liza**  You have a fine voice, Liam – it came back to you.

**Liam**  But not my nerve. Not that. I can sing among friends – family, but not in public, not with strangers, not even at Mass. Tell her why.

**Triona**  She might not want –

**Liam**  My voice broke at Mass, Christmas Mass, singing 'Adeste Fidelis'. One boy soprano chosen every year. That year, me. And in front of everybody I stopped. I opened my mouth and never heard the sound before. Not sweet – not soaring – but as if a wasp had stung my tongue, paralysing it. The choir stood up, and they finished the hymn. That's what I got for being the centre of attention, I just wanted the ground to swallow me. Why did God let that happen?

**Liza**  It's biology, Liam – just growing up – a boy's voice –

**Liam** Deepens – I know that – no, I mean why let it happen at Christmastime at Mass. It was a sore temptation to stop believing in Him. Why single me out for special chastisement? But I kept the faith. I did – I had to –

**Liza** So has Jackie.

**Liam** What?

*Triona bursts out laughing.*

**Triona** That heathen – what makes you think that?

**Liam** He surely doesn't claim he's Gospel-greedy?

**Triona** The pagan's forgotten how to say his prayers, if he ever knew any. This will stun my father and mother. Jolly Jackie beats his breasts at the altar rails now? Has he recalled where to locate them? To see him on his knees – you could sell tickets to watch that miracle.

**Liam** I'm not one to preach nor throw stones, but I'd doubt there's much truth in Mr Jackie Day's conversion –

**Liza** I'm telling you the truth.

**Liam** Prove it.

**Liza** Not soon, but somewhere down the road, he's toying with the idea he'll make an album singing duets with Christian singers and musicians.

*Triona squeals.*

**Triona** I knew one day he'd turn into Van Morrison.

**Liza** There is a very large, very serious market for music like that –

**Triona** Or even the next Cliff Richard –

**Liam** Has he sunk so low?

**Triona** She is pulling our leg.

**Liam** No, she is not.

**Liza** You're right – I'm not.

*Silence.*

**Triona** Was it your hope he'd go down this direction?

*Silence.*

**Liam** He can't do that.

**Triona** Hence the talk of getting hitched?

**Liam** He cannot mock God.

**Triona** The loving couple, rhapsodising together?

**Liam** He will go to hell.

**Triona** The happy marriage of the reformed sinner and the woman who saved him. A perfect sell.

**Liza** I said there was a market – more correct to say there is a need –

**Triona** I will expose the pair of you –

**Liza** A hunger for –

**Triona** Lies. Filthy, foul, fuckable lies.

**Liza** Are you going to stop him?

**Triona** No, he's a grown man. How could I stop him? But he's my brother and I can smell when he's peddling forty shades of shite, and this is it.

**Liam** God won't allow it. He won't abandon all –

**Triona** Liam, would you ever realise something? God doesn't so much abandon your like as grab you by the

84

balls and fling you away over his shoulders. A very
private, precious wound between your legs. It's why we
have no kids. All God's fault. Not mine. Not yours. His.
Console yourself with that lie. It's what consoles me.

**Liam** Then you're no better than Jackie if that's all you
believe.

**Liza** What do you believe?

**Liam** At Mass I go and receive a piece of bread, a drink
of wine – that bread, wine is the body and blood of
Christ, my saviour. I believe I am in communion with
Him and the saints. I believe in that, because if I didn't,
what more have I? How else can I make sense of my life?
I believe in Christ because He lets me live. I could not go
on without Him. Laugh at me if you like. Mock – mock
me. That is all I have going. It's all I want. For I am a
man who sees miracles every day. That's enough. I don't
try to work them.

**Liza** If you could work a miracle –

**Liam** What would it be? Look at us, the two of us – isn't
it crystal clear? And if I can't have a child, I'd ask for
what to me is as good – that we be content with each
other, even without. But I can't see either happening.

*Silence.*
    *Triona goes to Liam and kisses him, a kiss he
returns passionately.*

*Fade.*


SCENE SIX

*Song, Liza and Irene sing in duet 'The Map of the
World', then Jackie joins in.*

85

### Liza / Irene

I touch you, carved from the hardest ice,
Hands that don't feel, heart that can't beat.
I see the map of the world in your face,
The map of the world where no roads meet.
Why must you always speak in forked tongue
Secrets and shadows, of loss and of pain?
Why leave our bed when the night is young?
The map of the world turns to ice again.

### Jackie

A woman knows when a man's carved from ice,
He lets it cover the map of the world.
She reads his lies in the lines of her face,
She bides her time, she sees it unfurl
When he must always speak in forked tongue
The secrets and shadows, the loss and the pain
When he leaves her while the night is young –
And the map of the world turns to ice again.
Map of the world. Map of the world.

### Liza / Irene

Touch me now this hardest ice.
My hands can feel, my heart can beat.
Show me the map of the world in your face,
The map of the world where all roads meet.
Talk to me, give me the gift of tongues –
No secrets, no shadows, no loss and no pain,
Stay in our bed when the night is young.
The map of the world will be ours again.
Map of the world. Map of the world.

### Jackie

Touch me and melt this hardest ice.
My hands can feel, my heart can beat.
Show me the map of the world in your face,
The map of the world where all roads meet.
Talk to me, give me the gift of tongues –

No secrets, no shadows, no loss, no pain,
Stay in our bed when the night is young.
The map of the world will be ours again.
Map of the world. Map of the world.
Map of the world. Map of the world

*Jackie strums his guitar.*

**Hugo** There's worse things to be than dead, you know.

**Jackie** You're not dead.

**Hugo** Did I say I was?

*Jackie continues strumming the guitar, not answering.*

You could go to a funeral and bury a corpse, and you might think it's the stiff you should feel sorry for, but remember this, there might be somebody standing still drawing breath, and that man or woman might still be breaking their heart in love with whoever is in the coffin, inconsolable because they never uttered a word of this to a living soul, and now it's too late.

*Jackie strums on the guitar.*

So, I rest my case – there's worse things to be than dead.

**Jackie** Why don't you just tell her?

**Hugo** Tell who? Tell what?

**Jackie** Tell her you fancy her – my grandmother.

**Hugo** Magdalene? That bad bitch – ride her? Young fella, have you lost your reason? Risk a leg over with that rough piece of work? That witch is old enough to be my wife. No connection at all – you've taken me up entirely wrongly. Do you not know who I refer to –

**Jackie** It's not my mother, surely?

**Hugo** Irene? She's spit out of your granny's mouth. She'd eat me as soon as laugh at me. And what kind of boyo do you think I am, my tongue hanging out for my son's wife?

*He blesses himself.*

You're off the mark there. Not your mother – but you're warm. Her sister – your aunt –

**Jackie** Joanne?

**Hugo** That's her. Would I have a chance in that quarter?

**Jackie** No, you wouldn't.

**Hugo** Don't be so sure, big head. You haven't all the women after you. There's space for a few of us.

**Jackie** Strange as it may seem, I'm not after my aunt. That's not why I'd say your chances –

**Hugo** Are slim?

**Jackie** Not a hope.

**Hugo** May I ask why you're so sure?

**Jackie** She never married, Joanne – she's fussy.

**Hugo** But she's getting no younger – maybe by now she's desperate.

**Jackie** That's a good line to use with any woman. I'd say the ladies would fall at your feet if you try that –

**Hugo** The last place I want her is at my feet. At my age how in Jesus would I lift her? It's a woman I'm looking for, not a crane –

**Jackie** You might have more future with a crane –

**Hugo** Have I? Well, I've seen the way she looks at me.

**Jackie** She can hardly not look at you – you rarely leave the house.

**Hugo** So we're well used to each other – a good sign. She told me once I'd sicken a goat. You know what they get up to, goats –

**Jackie** Go no further down that road.

**Hugo** What should I do then? What would you, the young buck, advise –

**Jackie** I would leave my aunt to her own devices, and so should you. You'll be carried to your grave with your secret intact. I won't say a word.

**Hugo** That's big of you, but who's to say you won't go before me?

**Jackie** Who indeed?

**Hugo** I mean you hear all sorts of stories about America and all those places out foreign you've been touring, riddled with every strange disease under the sun. Christ knows what you picked up in your bed. Who can say what you could come down with years before me or your aunt?

**Jackie** Your good heart becomes you.

**Hugo** I might outlast you. Not that you should envy my long life. Our backs are against the wall. Sure, what have we been telling you? Aren't you here to heed your daddy's worries? Isn't it as well I've been putting a few shillings aside. Nothing fancy folk like yourselves could squander, just a small harvest. It might tempt your aunt Joanne, should she like the rest be evicted to the side of the road. It would force her to decide taking me isn't the roughest of stations. There's my son – he'll tell us if she's fussy.

*He has seen Conor approach.*

**Conor** What plans are you hatching?

**Hugo** Sharing some secrets, weren't we, Jackie boy? I was just listening to him play his lovely guitar, bringing my head peace.

**Jackie** You were indeed, Grandpa.

**Hugo** Would you listen to him, calling myself Grandpa. Hasn't he turned very Yankee indeed?

**Jackie** What would you prefer I called you? Is there another name might be more appropriate?

**Hugo** Isn't he the right swank – appropriate? Could we be up to him? He'll turn his back on us completely soon. Who could blame him? We never give him any credit for all he's earned.

**Conor** Jackie's a down-to-earth lad.

**Hugo** Too modest he is – we let him be. Tell them who you are, boy – how they look up to you outside this country. It's no good respecting a fellow only when you're coming with your hand out to him. Amn't I right, Conor, my son?

**Conor** Aren't you always, Father?

**Hugo** Father and son, in perfect harmony. You could sing that if you put a tune to it, but I won't try. Sure I haven't a note in my head.

**Jackie** You said it, Grandpa.

**Hugo** Isn't there a song called 'I'm My Own Grandpa'? Somebody marries a widow who turns out to have wed his grandfather who himself has been hitched and divorced six times before – or was that the widow? Turns out he's now his own grandpa. Could you be up to the perversity of people? Adios, partners.

*He exits.*

**Conor** Sly fucker, that father of mine.

**Jackie** Aren't we all?

**Conor** What was the old goat looking for?

**Jackie** You think he's a goat?

**Conor** He was once upon a time a dirty beast. Not a picture hall in Donegal but he was barred from – no woman safe in the dark with him. Then he turned to daylight invasions. They threatened to have him doctored. Of course he next put the hand up the wrong colleen. Her father and uncles – she was an only child, no brothers, the goat knew that, but her menfolk rose to the bait. They waylaid him. Left the bastard for dead. Took about two years to recover.

**Jackie** And you did not retaliate?

**Conor** Happened well before I was conceived. Family secret, soon spilt. Nobody lifted a finger for him. It put manners on him. He married, and rarely strayed. People tend to forget what men get up to when they're young.

**Jackie** Would you say so?

**Conor** And Irene's family, when I married into it, they never threw it in his face. They were kind to him, forgetful as I said. Your mother, she was gentlest of all. What I'm trying to tell you is she's not the tight bitch you claim she is –

**Jackie** I didn't call her a tight bitch.

**Conor** Then what do you call her? The slippers song, what does it –

**Jackie** Who says it's about her?

**Conor** The dogs in the street, if you played it to them. That cut her to the quick. Was it meant to?

**Jackie** Da, what business is that of yours? Or hers, for that matter?

**Conor** What did you come home for? Is it only to keep hating –

**Jackie**  Why do you want me here? Are you well? Is she? I know Hugo is frail as an army tank. Magdalene seems to be thriving. The rest as always live on their nerves. So what is it?

**Conor**  You tell me, you're such a damned know-it-all. Always were, still are, always will be.

**Jackie**  Welcome back, Jackie – welcome home. Shake hands with all the neighbours, kiss the colleens all, you're as welcome as the flowers in May, to dear old Donegal.

**Conor**  Is that the best you can rise to about your home?

*Jackie plays and sings his own song, 'Donegal'.*

**Jackie**
I was born somewhere foreign
In a fort in a storm.
I was born in wind and rain,
I did the earth some harm.
All my days I've been searching
For shelter, for a song,
All my days spent on the wing
Trying to right a wrong.
In a place I never travelled,
Never heard of, never seen,
To a town of chiming bells
I glimpsed twice in a dream.
Tell me, what's this parish called –
Is it my home?
Tell me, what's this parish called,
Is it my home, my Donegal?

Mother, father, sister, brother,
Did you once create me?
Sister, brother, father, mother,
Listen and set me free.

I am flesh and bone and bondage,
Mountain, rock, running stream,
A bird that's left its gilded cage,
Hearing the earth's great keen,
For a place I never travelled,
Never heard of, never seen,
To a town of chiming bells,
I glimpsed twice in a dream.
Tell me, what's this parish called –
Is it my home?
Tell me, what's this parish called,
Is it my home, my Donegal?

Where's the fort long abandoned,
Somewhere foreign, somewhere near?
The battle's lost, the battle's won,
Somewhere you learned to fear?
Hold my hand in wind and rain,
In this fort, in a storm.
Lead me back from somewhere foreign,
Let me do the earth no harm,
To a place I've never travelled,
Never heard of, never seen,
To a town of chiming bells,
I glimpsed twice in a dream.
Tell me, what's this parish called –
Is it my home?
Tell me, what's this parish called,
Is it my home, my Donegal?

*There is a silence at the song's end.*

**Conor**  That sounds like a winner.

**Jackie**  Who can tell?

**Conor**  Did you write it recently?

**Jackie**  It's been brewing for a while.

**Conor**  How long?

**Jackie**  All my life.

**Conor**  You'd be reluctant to let it go? Hand it to another singer? Give it to your mother?

*Jackie suddenly howls. It is not a mocking sound, but something terrifying, despairing, and shocks Conor.*

What in Christ's name was that in aid of?

**Jackie**  Why not just ask me for money?

**Conor**  Who says I need money?

**Jackie**  Let me put my hand in my pocket.

**Conor**  Keep whatever's there – I've no need –

**Jackie**  Damn you, ask me for cash –

**Conor**  Where did you get this idea? We are managing, mister. Who put other in your head? More than managing –

**Jackie**  Da, how long have you got to keep things afloat?

**Conor**  A matter of weeks, if our luck lasts.

**Jackie**  Weeks?

**Conor**  Days, maybe longer –

**Jackie**  Days?

**Conor**  Maybe it's too late already. It's my fault – not hers. I keep it from her we're struggling to survive. She must see how few show their face at her gigs, but I tell her how I pull strings and cut costs –

**Jackie**  Who is earning in this house?

**Conor**  She is. I am.

**Jackie** When she makes money, you do, yes? Joanne –

**Conor** Keeps the house, helps your mother, as good as gold, Joanne.

**Jackie** Triona –

**Conor** Helps out at times in the bar and restaurant. Not great with the paying customers. Does the books. The accounts.

**Jackie** Has she ever switched on a computer?

**Conor** Not the most numerate, I acknowledge, but she's great with wigs –

**Jackie** My mother doesn't wear one –

**Conor** If she needs to ever, Triona's ready.

**Jackie** And Liam?

**Conor** Dependent on Triona – his nerves won't let him. Work.

**Jackie** One person keeps this entire show on the road. My mother? Jesus, you are a useless – utterly useless bastard, Father.

**Conor** I have served your mother well.

**Jackie** You've squandered everything she's earned, made a shambles of all she's done, and the stupid bitch would still say, thanks, Conor, thanks.

**Conor** What do you mean, squandered?

**Jackie** Spent it on yourself and on all surrounding you, so you get the credit you save them from the big bad world, where they'd go under without you – correction, it's you who'd first go under, useless bastard as I called you, useless as you are –

**Conor**  This all stems from me asking you for one lousy song – let your mother have it. This is my answer, this torrent of abuse. I'll ask for no more –

**Jackie**  Wait a minute – what do you mean by that 'no more'? Nothing, but nothing, Father, is ever simple with you. What is that soft, sweet mouth begging for? It's not one song you want, is it?

**Conor**  A whole album. New songs. Duets, if you like. Mother and son mostly, but invite other big names. You two singing together, a new departure for the pair of you, appealing to –

**Jackie**  Who does she still appeal to? The dead in our cemetery? Will they rise from their graves to buy her records?

**Conor**  She reared you –

**Jackie**  Badly.

**Conor**  That's all too obvious. There were children had it worse. Were you left starving?

**Jackie**  You deserve to go under. I want you to go under.

**Conor**  You don't mean that, do you? Have you the money to save us? The whole clan's depending on you being the man they think you are, and I know you are. You won't refuse us, will you?

**Jackie**  It's common knowledge, is it, you're asking this? My mother –

**Conor**  Is an innocent party. She doesn't even know about the duets. That's all my thinking. She believes I've sought you out to complain you made a mockery of her in your song –

**Jackie**  Then why sing it as a duet?

**Conor**  Not the slipper song. I mean the Donegal one – she could do that justice, her home county.

**Jackie**  Does that word 'justice' not stick in your gullet?

**Conor**  I've done my best, boy.

**Jackie**  And that's about as bad as I can say of you.

**Conor**  Are you telling me to go to hell? You won't save –

**Jackie**  What's in it for me if –

**Conor**  You spare us the shame of eviction, spare yourself –

**Jackie**  I'll be up and gone and far away.

**Conor**  Why did you come back?

**Jackie**  Because you asked.

**Conor**  And you're here. We are who you come from. We are who you'll go to. We are there with you, come hell or high water. I fed and clothed you. I did not begrudge you a penny. This is the first thing I have asked from you.

**Jackie**  And the last.

**Conor**  Your final word?

**Jackie**  Maybe. Wait and see. The restaurant goes. The bar goes. Get as good a price as you can swindle for them. Use Ma's name. Use my name to inflate what they're worth. Agree to that – we'll talk more.

**Conor**  Joanne could manage them – earn her keep. Don't say a word to your mother – she knows nothing.

**Jackie**  She knows everything.

*Irene enters.*

97

**Irene** Well, have you asked him? Any word of saying sorry –

**Conor** He can tell you better than I can.

**Irene** I don't know if I should break breath to him.

**Conor** I can't help you there – that business is between the two of you. I'm off.

**Jackie** Running off again, eh, Da?

**Irene** Doesn't he always?

**Jackie** Always and ever – no argument there – spares himself all fights.

**Irene** No argument whatsoever.

**Conor** Isn't it grand to see the two of you so pleasant together? Delightful as that may be, I won't stick around to be either of your whipping boy any longer. As they say in the best old songs, adios, amigos.

*He looks Irene straight in the eye.*

He's your son. Deal with him. I've done what I can.

*Conor exits.*

**Jackie** So you do know everything. I guessed as much.

**Irene** It must be great to be a good guesser.

**Jackie** I'd say I was more than that.

**Irene** Would you? What then – what are you?

**Jackie** My mother's son.

**Irene** You must love yourself today then.

**Jackie** I do. What about your good self?

**Irene** Me? Do I love you –

98

**Jackie** I know the reply to that. No need to follow on. No, I was inquiring do you love yourself today, Mother? Do you mind me calling you that? Or would Mammy better suit your ears? Will we try Mama? Mama – Mama – Mama. Which would you like me to bleat at you?

**Irene** Mother will suffice.

**Jackie** Then allow me, Mother, to repeat my original sin – I meant, original question: do you love yourself today?

**Irene** The sight of myself – the sound?

**Jackie** The sight, the sound.

**Irene** I can't say I do – every sound is drowned out.

**Jackie** What by? The wind – the rain – the big bad sea? The fierce Atlantic Ocean, engulfing Donegal, sweeping far into sweet oblivion all who do reside on this shore and shingle. Is that what drowns you out?

**Irene** No.

**Jackie** Is that what drags you here – no point resisting –

**Irene** Nothing like that. Something scarier.

**Jackie** What? Who?

**Irene** A boy. A boy I knew once. He fills me with dread.

**Jackie** Who was the boy?

**Irene** I taught him once upon a time. Taught him to sing.

**Jackie** And did he learn?

**Irene** Did he need to? He opened his mouth – what came out of it?

**Jackie** Tell me.

**Irene** Something shocking.

**Jackie** Something terrible.

**Irene** Yes, and strange too.

**Jackie** What way?

**Irene** Beautiful. Beyond compare. A voice to shatter glass. Pure. Better – a voice better than I was – than I had ever been. Better than I would ever be.

**Jackie** Did he know that?

**Irene** He didn't. How could he? He was a child.

**Jackie** Did you tell –

**Irene** Tell him what?

*Silence.*

That I couldn't listen? Couldn't bear him? Out of sight I wanted him – out of sound. No listening, no looking. Silence him. His mother. I think she went mad. More than a little mad.

**Jackie** And there was none to help her?

**Irene** Perhaps entirely mad.

**Jackie** There was none to hear her?

**Irene** The jealous bitch.

**Jackie** No.

**Irene** The selfish fucker. The cruel mother.

**Jackie** No, never cruel.

**Irene** Now, why should he save her, the child rejected? Why forgive her, the boy she would have broken?

**Jackie** He didn't break, did he? For he came from her. But he needs to ask, what possessed her?

**Irene** Who can say for sure, but there was revenge. Who by? Who knows, but from then on, when she opened her mouth to sing, all pleasure drained from any music she made. It was just a job, a chore, a day's long work, morning till night.

**Jackie** She deserved that, I think.

**Irene** So do I. She deserved all she got. Slap it into her, I hear you say. And I'd agree. Does that content you?

**Jackie** Da wants me to save your skin.

**Irene** Hearing me admit this, might that stop you hating?

**Jackie** He wants me to fork out for all your debts.

**Irene** Because it's eating him up, the debt.

**Jackie** He wants me to provide for you, now I can well afford it.

**Irene** Why should you?

**Jackie** He wants us to record a duet – Sing with me – will you?

**Irene** Sing what?

**Jackie** A song of mine, about Donegal.

**Irene** I don't know it.

**Jackie** It's just written – how could you? I would need to teach you, as you taught me.

**Irene** There's a dangerous precedent.

**Jackie** I'll risk the danger. Will you? Will we go back in time?

**Irene** Back in time – to when I lost you?

**Jackie** I was thinking more of back in time like *Doctor Who*, watching it long ago when we were, we were –

**Irene** What were we?

**Jackie** Tell me. What? Was it together?

**Irene** Sometimes, I suppose. Yourself. Myself.

**Jackie** Ourselves. Sometimes.

**Irene** Watching it, *Doctor Who* –

**Jackie** Together.

*They chant the electronic intro to 'Doctor Who'.*

**Irene** What place are we, Doctor?

**Jackie** Here – in this place – Donegal, I can't say when.

**Irene** The Ice Age?

**Jackie** Later.

**Irene** The Stone Age?

**Jackie** Later.

**Irene** Do they speak English?

**Jackie** No, something else. Something earlier. Latin, yes, Latin.

**Irene** Latin?

**Jackie** For sure – listen.

*Jackie starts to sing 'Panis Angelicus'.*

Panis angelicus,
fit panis hominum;
Dat panis coelicus
figuris terminum.

*He stops.*

Mother, sing with me. Teach me.

**Irene** I can't, Jackie.

**Jackie** You can.

*They sing in duet.*

**Duet**
O res mirabilis!
Manducat Dominum
Pauper, pauper servus et humilis.

**Irene** No more.

**Jackie** Together.

*They sing in duet to the hymn's conclusion.*

**Duet**
Te trina Deitas
unaque poscimus;
Sic nos tu visita
sicut te colimus.
Per tuas semitas
duc nos quo tendimus,
Ad lucem quam inhabitas.
Ad lucem quam inhabitas.

*Silence.*
*Liza appears out of the darkness.*

**Liza** My lord, the Von Trapp family making harmonies.
I hope I haven't spoilt the sing-along. If I knew there was
a party, I'd have worn a pretty dress. But I should not be
cross. I guess you're rehearsing for the –

**Jackie** For the pile of pious crap you think I'm mad
enough to be talked into? What makes you think I need

that? What makes you think you could do that? Who do you think you are?

**Liza** Someone who cares about you – cares enough to get you away from here. When do you say we leave – have you any idea?

**Irene** Why leave?

**Liza** Tight schedules. People depend on us.

**Irene** To be reliable. That's nice. Was that how I reared you? Or rather, why I did not rear you? Are you reliable, Jackie? Are you to be trusted?

**Liza** He is. Now.

**Irene** Not once upon a time.

**Liza** That time is gone.

**Irene** Break up her brother's marriage, Jackie.

**Liza** Why would he do that?

**Irene** Because he can.

**Liza** When do we leave, Jackie?

*Silence.*

A few days?

**Jackie** You don't get it, do you?

**Liza** Get what?

**Jackie** You don't speak the language.

**Liza** I think I do.

**Jackie** In your dreams.

**Liza** Maybe.

**Jackie** Then dream on. Leave, you leave.

*Silence.*

Just leave, I'll stay.

*He walks away, turning to his mother.*

Thanks – for the song.

*Jackie leaves.*

**Irene** We're like the weather in this part of the world. Changeable, never knowing what's coming next – Donegal. Part of its charm. And as for strangers, they're never at home here. It happens a lot. Being left. Or let go. Do as he warns you. Disappear.

**Liza** You won't win him.

**Irene** I'm not trying. There's no contest. He's made his choice. He did years ago. If you won't know that, you know nothing. And you do, don't you? Know nothing –

**Liza** Jack –

**Irene** Run after him.

**Liza** Jackie –

**Irene** Catch him if you – catch Jackie – catch him.

*Liza runs off, and Irene laughs after her.*
*She hums a few bars of 'Panis Angelicus'.*

*Fade.*

### SCENE SEVEN

*A boy soprano, somewhere from the past, haunts the house, singing a piece of 'Panis Angelicus'.*
*Cases packed, ready to go.*
*Joanne stands smoking, a glass of orange juice in her hand.*
*Hugo enters.*

**Hugo** She's packed and ready to go – he won't be seeing her off?

**Joanne** Not to the best of my knowledge.

**Hugo** She had a very short stay, didn't she? Not even seeing her to the station – why?

**Joanne** Aren't you the right quizmaster this morning? Gather your information from either of the two people involved. I have no news for you.

**Hugo** Nothing escapes your ears and eyes.

**Joanne** Says who?

**Hugo** The world.

**Joanne** Then who am I to contradict the world?

**Hugo** You never stop, do you, Joanne?

**Joanne** I suppose I never do.

**Hugo** Aren't you ever tired – worn out – exhausted?

**Joanne** Not in the slightest.

**Hugo** Such energy. How do you mind the house and mind us all as well?

**Joanne** I sleep sound in my own bed. Nothing or no one to disturb me.

**Hugo** How would they manage without you?

**Joanne** Exceedingly well. I may be wrong, but what I think you'd like to ask is how would I manage without them?

**Hugo** How would you?

**Joanne** For me to know – for you to find out.

**Hugo**  I wouldn't mind that. Finding out – if you'd let me. Can you read the writing on the wall here as well? You're no fool – you must have. One wage coming in, and it severely depleted. Even if my grandson does the decent thing and bails them out, how long can that last? This is a going concern no longer. Look at you, lighting a cigarette from the one you're already smoking.

**Joanne**  You could take me nowhere.

**Hugo**  How much are they now, ten – twenty cigarettes?

**Joanne**  I wouldn't know.

**Hugo**  You bought them.

**Joanne**  Not really – I robbed a sweetie shop, just for the fags. Hard times on the horizon, as you yourself say. All hands need get used to handling a gun.

**Hugo**  You'll always find somebody to mind you, a strapping lass –

**Joanne**  I prefer to use the gun over the strap – what about you?

**Hugo**  You've lost me there –

**Joanne**  Which would you prefer? Beaten to death by a strap or a bullet in the head from my gun? I ask that because you'll be dead in the earth before I look twice at you, listening to your little jokes, you letting on you're innocent, while your heart is one big act of begrudgery.

**Hugo**  I was only going to invite –

**Joanne**  Don't –

**Hugo**  Invite you out to have a bite with me?

**Joanne**  Taste this.

*She gives him the orange juice, and he chokes, tasting it.*

**Hugo** What the hell's in here?

**Joanne** Orange juice.

**Hugo** What else? Vodka? At this hour in the morning?

**Joanne** Precisely. That's what I'm downing, the woman you ask out for a bite, and here's my answer. I can just about keep up appearances to let on this is juice alone I'm drinking. Were I to take up your kind offer, they would need to dig me out of the open bottle. Damn you, I'm not sunk as low as to need you. I've already given to charity.

**Hugo** I've a bit of money saved –

**Joanne** Spend it.

**Hugo** On you. It would be enough for us two, should anything befall –

**Joanne** You will never, ever befall me.

**Hugo** You weren't always that proud. Don't think because I didn't tell, I didn't see –

**Joanne** See what? Tell what? What's your big secret?

**Hugo** My son, you and him – why he's put up with you. Why she has, your sister, why you're let live here. You're no more than his fancy woman. She allows it, Irene. You and her, your family – dirt incarnate. Filth you are, and you've turned my son into what you are, what my queer grandson – what you made him – filth, fucking filth.

**Joanne** There is filth here, but it is you. No, I'm wrong. Why give you the satisfaction of thinking you're right? That's not what are you. You are old – an old man. A lonely old man. And you deserve to be.

**Hugo** Drown in booze. Die.

*He races off, nearly colliding with Liza.*

Get out of my road.

**Liza**  Charming – What's your rush – what's got into him?

**Joanne**  Irish men – like that when they don't get the leg over. But I presume that's not why you abandon us. Quite the opposite, I dare say, if I may be blunt?

**Liza**  Be what you want to be. It's of no concern to me any more.

**Joanne**  Jackie's not out of bed yet –

**Liza**  He can be dead in his bed.

**Joanne**  Things go awry.

**Liza**  Would you say so? Is that the consolation I carry from the old soil?

**Joanne**  Why are you looking for it?

**Liza**  Consolation? Just a word. Words. Empty words. Have you ordered a cab?

**Joanne**  As you asked – and you want to go on your own?

**Liza**  Absolutely – all alone.

**Joanne**  So you're going away, with no word of farewell.

**Liza**  No farewell. No need. We didn't ever make it as far as hello, me and him, if we tell the truth.

**Joanne**  That would be a change in this house.

**Liza**  Why do you do it to each other –

**Joanne**  Maul the daylights –

**Liza**  Not even that. Not as clean as that.

**Joanne** Maybe we were better when we drank and smoked ourselves stupid. Maybe I say that because I'm keeping up the side here.

**Liza** Maybe that's why I could have talked to you –

**Joanne** But you haven't –

**Liza** What matter now.

**Joanne** When we were addicts – each and every one – we were simpler. Happier, even. A bunch of peasants, blasting our brains out on whatever concoction we could forge out of potatoes. Turning every pain into a pantomime. Looking to boo all the old villains. But who are they, now England's down and out? Who should we blame for our present woes? Will it ever be ourselves? We'd flog our souls as quickly as we'd swipe the green flag wrapped round us. We no longer own the shirts on our backs. Sold, to beat the band. Still, what else could you expect? A nation of nobodies, weeping into our overflowing glasses. Yes, our good selves, ourselves alone. Cheers.

*She raises her glass and downs its contents.*

What are you going back to?

**Liza** Myself.

**Joanne** Better than you'll find here. By the way, he had no intention, Jackie –

**Liza** But I had. That's the thing. I had. What's wrong with me?

*The taxi horn sounds.*

I had hopes.

**Joanne** Abandon it, abandon hope.

**Liza** Maybe you're right.

**Joanne** I am never right. What will I tell him?

**Liza** Make up something.

*Liza exits, and Joanne sits alone, humming 'Love Is Teasing'. Conor enters and joins in a part of the song.*

**Joanne** (*sings*)
For love is teasing and love is pleasing
And love is a pleasure when first it's new
But as it grows older then love grows colder
And fades away like the morning dew.

**Conor** You're up with the break of day.

**Joanne** (*sings*)
I wished, I wished, oh I wished in vain
I wished I was a maid again
But a maid again I can no more be
Than apples grow on an orange tree.

**Conor** He's done the necessary, Jackie, but unless you'd take over their running, he wants rid of both restaurant and pub.

**Joanne** (*sings*)
There is an alehouse in the town
And there my love he sits him down
He takes a strange girl on his knee
And he tells her things he once told me.

**Conor** He's not dictating who we leave the house to, he's not asking we sign it over to him, but Triona better know.

**Joanne** (*sings*)
For love and porter make a young girl older
And love and whiskey make her old and grey
And what cannot be cured, love, must be endured, love
And now I am bound for Amerikay.

**Conor**  Will you tell her the score? It might be easier coming from you –

**Joanne** (*sings*)
  But as love grows older then love grows colder
  And it fades away like the morning dew.

**Conor**  Are you making the breakfast?

**Joanne**  I'm not, no. And if Jackie wants rid of me –

**Conor**  I didn't repeat that –

**Joanne**  Run your pub and restaurant on top of skivvying here? I'm not singing for my supper, nor for yours either, Conor. You did business without consultation – don't ask for it now – deal with your own daughter.

  *She exits, singing.*

  As love grows older, love grows colder –

  *Conor watches her leave, then opens his paper and reads.*
    *Triona and Liam enter.*

**Triona**  She's left already, Liza?

**Conor**  So Joanne reports.

**Liam**  A bit abrupt. They're like that, Yanks. Don't get what they want – off they go.

**Triona**  So what did she want?

**Liam**  Your brother – I suppose. His money – his music.

**Triona**  Much like ourselves then. Will he deliver?

**Conor**  He has.

**Triona**  Bully for him.

**Liam**  We'll kill the fattened calf.

**Triona** No need. He won't expect that much. Remember, he's now a saint, this modest, blue-eyed boy.

**Conor** Why the temper?

**Triona** Who says I'm in a temper – I'll be like you – lie down and take it.

**Conor** He's giving us a hand –

**Triona** He's ruling the roost.

**Conor** He has the means – have you?

**Liam** Don't throw that in her face –

**Triona** Has Ma agreed –

**Conor** They're to sing together –

**Triona** He's won hands down again. He's beaten us.

**Conor** Nobody's beaten –

**Triona** She is, I am, you are. Jesus, have we any pride in ourselves?

**Conor** Listen to who's talking – listen to yourself.

**Triona** I am listening – but don't let me stop you – Off you lurk, happy as Larry.

*Conor is gone.*

**Liam** Stop upsetting yourself.

**Triona** And let him write a wee song all about me?
He's done it to everyone else. Am I not entitled to expect
I should be the next laughing stock?

*Jackie enters.*

**Jackie** Where's Liza? She's off?

**Triona** What's it like, Jackie? To be always right? Have all hands trembling talking to you? Something I'd like you to know –

**Liam** Not everyone here is frightened of you.

**Triona** To prove that, can you guess what I'm going to do? I will stop – just stop having anything more to do with you. Big deal, eh?

**Liam** More than he might think.

**Triona** I turn my back on all you do. You've done well, you deserve what you worked hard for, but you haven't got everything. I'm out of your life. That's all I can do to hurt you, as you hurt me. You've lost me.

**Jackie** Long ago.

**Liam** Not long enough.

**Triona** How much more do you intend hanging around here?

**Jackie** As my humour dictates.

*Irene enters.*

**Irene** You're up with the lark.

**Triona** Me a lark? Sure I haven't a note in my head. That's for you and him.

**Irene** Why have you a face on you?

**Triona** Fuck off, Mother.

**Irene** Excuse me? What did I do to deserve –

**Triona** The worst word in my stomach? I'll tell you. He saves us, you let him.

**Irene** Why shouldn't I?

**Triona**  He walks over us. He rules the roost.

**Liam**  No matter what he's done and is doing with his life, home is the hero and all is forgiven.

**Triona**  Well, he's yours entirely. I'm out of here till he does a runner once more. Why don't you just go with him? Piss off, the pair of you. We might all be better off.

*She leaves.*

**Liam**  She means it – you've lost her.

**Jackie**  You'll look after her, I'm sure.

**Liam**  I will. She has someone beside her. Have you? No, and you never will. As for your music? Have we not all heard it somewhere before? Not a note your own – all of it, stolen. What is it they call your like? Plagiarist. I wouldn't let my wife be soiled by such company.

*Liam exits.*

**Irene**  His wife will be back. Tail between her legs. Whinging. What has she got going for her but her temper? Let her keep it.

**Jackie**  And she has him. He's loyal. Lucky Triona.

**Irene**  The Yank has gone?

**Jackie**  With the wind.

**Irene**  Will you follow her?

**Jackie**  Maybe.

**Irene**  That's a no, then?

**Jackie**  I always say maybe.

**Irene**  You always say no, son. Will we do this duet?

**Jackie** Maybe – no – yes.

**Irene** Thank you. You'll hang around for another while?

**Jackie** If you ask me.

**Irene** I do.

**Jackie** Where's the grandmother?

**Irene** Joanne's getting her ready.

**Jackie** How much longer has she got?

**Irene** Your grandmother? I'd say –

**Jackie** No, I mean Joanne.

**Irene** What are you saying about my sister?

*Silence.*

Has she told you something she hasn't said to me? What are you warning, Jackie?

**Jackie** Look at her – listen to her – she's a tired woman, very tired.

**Irene** And I'm not?

**Jackie** You're not, no. You're like Magdalene. Nothing will shift you. Nothing will kill you.

**Irene** And my sister?

**Jackie** She is getting ready to kill herself.

**Irene** We don't do things like that –

**Jackie** We've started.

**Irene** This is Donegal.

**Jackie** This is everywhere.

*Joanne enters with Magdalene.*

116

**Magdalene** She has tugged what little hairs I have off my scalp. I nearly screamed with the agony. Did you not hear me?

**Joanne** How would they hear you if you only nearly screamed?

**Magdalene** Don't be so smart.

**Joanne** Will I make a late breakfast?

**Magdalene** I want nothing.

**Joanne** But others might – I might.

**Magdalene** Then eat your fill. Ignore me.

**Joanne** What do you want?

**Magdalene** A bit of sausage. A slice of bacon. Keep eggs from me. Maybe a bit of scrambled. Toast. Brown bread – I wouldn't thank you. White then. And tea. If you could spare it.

**Joanne** Is that it?

**Magdalene** Thanks. What's keeping you from cooking?

**Joanne** Jesus, this morning – this life.

*She exits.*

**Magdalene** Thought she would never leave. Nosy bitch. Look at you two, don't say you're plotting nothing. The pair of you, well-matched – one as capable as the other of knifing anyone unfortunate enough to be stuck between you, as I am. But do you know who I blame for this?

**Irene** Yourself.

**Magdalene** I do – I do blame myself. And maybe I should look and find forgiveness. You know me. Whose advice do I always follow? Bridie Gallagher – now that was a woman who could sing, I would listen to her. 'He could handle a spade and court a maid, as well as any man. How could you part and break the heart of the girl from Donegal?' Wasn't that my motto? No, think again. Yes, I have it now. Didn't that lassie from Creeshlough pour her heart out when she declared to the world, 'I'll forgive but I'll never forget.' Yes, that's it. 'I'll forgive, but I'll never forget.' Wait one minute though – I never forget, I never forgive. Fuck Bridie Gallagher.

**Irene** Poor Bridie – she died not that long ago, a very sad life. Didn't we send flowers to her funeral?

**Magdalene** Did she send them to mine?

**Jackie** You haven't had a funeral.

**Magdalene** Because it would be begrudged to me. You barely give me time of day. I look for a kind word, I'm given a stone. Why do I go on? If I ask, I'm always refused –

**Irene** What are you refused?

**Magdalene** A song. How long since I heard you sing together? Sing, the two of you. Sing.

*Jackie sings.*

**Jackie**
    Mother, father, sister, brother,
    Did you once create me?
    Sister, brother, father, mother,
    Listen and set me free.

*Irene sings.*

**Irene**
    I am flesh and bone and bondage
    Mountain, rock, running stream,
    A bird that's left its gilded cage,
    Hearing the earth's great keen.

*They sing together as Magdalene closes her eyes.*

**Jackie / Irene**
For a place I've never travelled,
Never heard of, never seen,
To a town of chiming bells
I glimpsed twice in a dream.
Tell me, what's this parish called –
Is it my home?
Tell me, what's this parish called –
Is it my home, my Donegal?

**Jackie** Grandmother?

*Silence.*

**Irene** Mother?

*Silence.*
*Magdalene opens her eyes.*

**Magdalene** Donegal.

*In fading light the company start to assemble and sing the first and third stanzas of 'Donegal'.*

**Company**
I was born somewhere foreign
In a fort in a storm.
I was born in wind and rain,
I did the earth some harm.
All my days I've been searching
For shelter, for a song,
All my days spent on the wing
Trying to right a wrong.
In a place I never travelled,
Never heard of, never seen,
To a town of chiming bells
I glimpsed twice in a dream.
Tell me, what's this parish called –

Is it my home?
Tell me, what's this parish called –
Is it my home, my Donegal?

Where's the fort long abandoned,
Somewhere foreign, somewhere near?
The battle's lost, the battle's won,
Somewhere you learn to fear?
Hold my hand in wind and rain
In this fort, in this storm.
Lead me back from somewhere foreign,
Let me do the earth no harm,
In a place I've never travelled,
Never heard of, never seen,
To a town of chiming bells,
I glimpsed twice in a dream.
Tell me, what's this parish called –
Is it my home?
Tell me, what's this parish called,
Is it my home, my Donegal?
My Donegal. My Donegal.

# The Music

**KEVIN DOHERTY**

*Arranged by Conor Linehan*

# Leaving Donegal

Frank McGuinness

Kevin Doherty

# Feasting on Freshness

Frank McGuinness

Kevin Doherty

55
wan-dere the streets of fair Am - ster-dam I felt `north Seas in my__ two palms

57
What did that ci-ty of dia- monds bring to my eyes and my ears but the shine_____ of

A#   A

E

60
herr-ing   Feast-ing on fresh-ness feast-ing on herr-ing

Bmin   Bmin

63
feast-ing on fresh-ness feast ing on herr - ing   Feast-ing on fresh-ness feast - ing on herr - ing

F

65
feast-ing on fresh-ness feast ing on herr-ing   Dance with me

A   A   A7   D

# Ladies in Waiting

Frank McGuinness

Kevin Doherty

4

wait -ing     Raise a glass    to the la - dies in    wait-ing        Good luck and cheers

good health and more    beers    Serve   us lad - ies in   wait - - ing

# Lullaby

Frank McGuinness

Kevin Doherty
arr. Conor Linehan

man in the moon looks in-to your eyes sleep sleep sleep child Birds of the air from par - a dise___

Sleep sleep sleep child The

man in the moon looks in - to your eyes

# Broken Glass Slippers

rank McGuinness

Kevin Doherty

Well I know a man who fell in love with a wom - an two hands in one glove

**A**

With rings on her fin - ers and bells on her toes Hav - ing mus - ic where - ev - er she goes_____ And I know a wom - an who

141

bare stock-inged feet

Boots_____ that could stamp on nak___ ed feet

Boots that could sha - - - - tter del - i-cate

glass_____ del - i-cate glass_____

glass                    Slipp-ers of  glass

know  a  fath - er who    loved  a  moth - er I   know   a   moth - er who

Frank McGuinness

# Green Light

Kevin Doherty

151

2

152

# Map of the World

Frank McGuinness

Kevin Doherty

I touch you carved from the hard - est ice

hands that don't feel____ heart that can't beat   I see the map of the world   in your face   The

map of the   world   where no   roads   meet   Why must you al-ways   speak in fork-ed   tongue

sec - rets and   sha_dow   of   loss and of   pain_   Why leave our bed____ when the

49

heart can beat   Show me the map   of the   world   in your face   The map of the world   where

D          D⁹          Bmin                    Bmin⁷          Bmin          D

53

all   roads   meet.        Talk   to me give me       the gift   of       tongues        no

D⁹                    Emin⁷                              Emin          Emin¹¹

56

sec - rets   no sha - dows       no loss and no   pain       Stay   in our bed       when the

D                              D⁹              Emin⁷

59

night is       young       and the map of the   world   will be ours a-gain

Emin¹¹          Emin⁷          A          A¹¹          A          A¹¹          A

# Donegal Finale

Frank McGuinness

Kevin Doherty